Quest for the Best

Also by Stanley Marcus
Minding the Store

Quest for the Best

Stanley Marcus

McGraw-Hill Book Company

New York   St. Louis   San Francisco   Bogotá   Guatemala
Hamburg   Lisbon   Madrid   Mexico   Montreal   Panama
Paris   San Juan   São Paulo   Tokyo   Toronto

First McGraw-Hill Paperback edition, 1985

Reprinted by arrangement with The Viking Press

1 2 3 4 5 6 7 8 9 DOC DOC 8 7 6 5

ISBN 0-07-040294-9

Library of Congress Cataloging in Publication Data

Marcus, Stanley, 1905–
    Quest for the best.

    Includes index.
        1. Marcus, Stanley, 1905–   2. Businessmen—
Biography.   3. Commercial products.   4. Quality of
products.   I. Title.
HF3023.M37A36   1985   381'.092'4 [B]   84-26168
ISBN 0-07-040294-9 (pbk.)

Page 228 constitutes an extension of the copyright page.

To Billie,
Who was the best

An Appreciation

My gratitude goes to Aaron Priest, my agent, for his enthusiastic support of the subject of this book; to Alice Snavely, my executive assistant, for her tireless efforts to keep it on schedule and free of errors; to Margaret Bradley for typing the manuscript; to Hortense Spitz, Wanda Lampier, Pam Proctor, and Doris McCallum for their many contributions; and, above all, to my late wife, Billie, who ungrudgingly provided me the freedom of time in which to write and who made valuable critical comments as the work progressed.

Preface

My first book, *Minding the Store,* was a memoir in which I related the genesis and growth of Neiman-Marcus and my own development as a merchant and a person. *Quest for the Best* is also a memoir, but of a different kind, one that deals with my experience in the pursuit of the BEST products and services, worldwide, over the past fifty years.

Having retired from a day-to-day participation in the retail business, I have been able to enjoy the opportunity of looking objectively at the changing methodology of the consumer industries and the people who operate them. Much of this was visible to me when I was a practicing retailer, although I am now able to see with greater clarity the power of economic forces on both manufacturing and distribution and the resultant effects on the quality of merchandise and service.

My criticism of certain contemporary trends should not be interpreted as a lament for the good old days—it should be regarded, rather, as an expression of my strong convictions that economic decay is as subject to correction as land erosion. If I have stepped on tender toes, I'm not sorry.

Man's cultural history gives evidence that he has the ability to perform, create, and produce artifacts of quality on a scale ranging from mediocre to best, in bad taste and good, and with craftsmanship from poor to superb. What, then, is the BEST? Is it measurable? What are the rewards to both the producer and user? How do changing economic conditions affect the quality standards of industry?

These are some of the questions I have explored and sought to ascertain. As a longtime searcher for and purveyor of the BEST, I hope to have come up with some of the answers.

Contents

Quest for the Best

Habit de Marchand Miroitier Lunettier.

Paris, Chez N. de Larmessin, Rue St Jacques, à la Pomme d'Or.   Avec Privil. du Roy.

The Death of Elegance

Funeral services for eighteenth-century ELEGANCE were held in the mid-twentieth century without fanfare or even any general cognizance of its occurrence by admirers. Death was attributed to a variety of causes, including the replacement of hand labor by machine production, the establishment of the minimum wage, high taxation, the overthrow of monarchical government, and inevitability. Most of the friends of ELEGANCE were unaware of the long illness that had preceded its death.

So might an obituary have read, if the press took the same notice of the decease of eras as it does of people. I know, because I was there.

My adult life has been spent in the pursuit and sale of the finest goods and services, so I am convinced there is a market for the best—and a growing one at that—despite constantly increasing prices. Furthermore, there has been a market for the best, the most elegant, since civilization began, as literature and the artifacts of earlier cultures testify.

Elegance, to me, is a summary word denoting the ultimate in beauty, craftsmanship, and quality—all put together with taste. Elegance suggests selectivity, fitness, and authority—whether in decoration, personal adornment, or manners. It is an achievement of an elite society which had sufficient leisure, wealth, and interest to devote its attention to living in tasteful luxury—be it the eighteenth-century French court or the royal family of Benin. This condition could occur only during periods of abundant cheap labor which could provide retinues of domestic servants and ample numbers of skilled craftsmen to fulfill their masters' demands for luxury articles.

The history of Western civilization is filled with many ages of elegance; the last one took place in the eighteenth and nineteenth centuries, and its end was foredoomed by the effects of the Industrial Revolution. Elegance, of course, is relative to the times and to the geographical location. What was elegant in the Egypt of Tutankhamen might not have been considered elegant by Marie Antoinette; what was elegant in Benin was different from what it was in nineteenth-century England. With the rise of the philosophy of democracy in western Europe, the concept of elitism became odious; as the machine age matured, we entered a period of less leisure, of broader distribution of wealth, and of the disappearance of cheap labor in the developed countries. Mass production provided an abundance of goods for the masses, but could find no place for the artisan-craftsman, who became a casualty of the revolution.

Years ago, I learned an important lesson on the subject of elegance from an experience I had on a visit to London. I had seen an Oriental rug in the window of a well-known dealer in Davies Street and my eye was attracted to it for its unusual design and color. I knew very little about Oriental rugs and I had never fully appreciated them. Fortunately, the gentleman who greeted me was the owner of the shop, and I shall always be grateful for the time he took to start my education. I introduced myself and told him that I had admired the rug in his window and asked its price and something of its history, admitting my complete ignorance about Oriental rugs.

After he had answered my questions, he asked if I would like to learn more about rugs. When I expressed an interest, he proceeded to show me some of his treasures. I admired an Ispahan, remarking, "This is an elegant rug."

"No, Mr. Marcus," he replied in his grave, dignified

manner, "if you will pardon me, it is fine, but not elegant. Here," he said, unrolling another rug of similar size, "is a marvelous Ispahan, one that is truly elegant. The first rug I showed you is made of wool with three hundred knots to the square inch. This second one has a silk warp with four hundred knots per square inch. One of the most fastidious noblemen in Persia commissioned this rug; he selected a weaver who was renowned for his skill and famous for the elegance of his work."

By this time I was impressed by his emphasis on the word "elegant." He continued: "Get on the floor, feel both rugs, and compare them. Also notice the fringe. It is indicative of how faithful the weaver was to himself by producing something of which he was proud."

I examined the two, and slowly my eyes perceived the differences between them. A few minutes before, I hadn't known what Ispahan meant—besides being the name of a city in Iran. Because this kind and knowledgeable man was willing to take the time to teach me, I had learned not only the reasons why one rug was fine but why the other was finer, more elegant. I went away pleased, not only by my recently acquired education but also by my new acquaintanceship with the idea of elegance, imparted by a man to whom the word had great significance. When I returned to Claridge's, I ran into the manager in the lobby and I asked him, "What makes this hotel so elegant?" Without batting an eye, he replied, "Our guests, of course."

The market for the elegant has always been a small percentage of the total population, because it has been limited to people of wealth. Not only does nature fail to provide unlimited quantities of the best, as in furs and diamonds, but man has often contributed to scarcity by restricting production out of prudence or cupidity. There is a greater risk in producing expensive articles, so it is good commercial judgment to keep supply and demand in close balance. Some producers deliberately create a market shortage to force higher prices. One maker of French lisle socks had a virtual monopoly on their production, making it necessary for buyers to place orders two years in advance of delivery. I asked

The Death of Elegance

why he didn't expand his production in order to give his customers faster service. He replied, "As it is, I can sit back with a comfortable backlog of orders. When business gets bad, my deliveries improve; I am able to deliver in one year. However, if I doubled the size of my plant and sales declined, I would have to hustle to keep the machines busy. I like it the way it is." Eventually, competition caught up with him, gave better deliveries and prices, and forced him out of business.

Rarity, caused by natural forces or by man, has been an attraction to wealthy buyers in the past even as it is today. There were grain speculators in Biblical times and tea and spice monopolists in fifteenth-century Venice; cardinals vied with each other for unique manuscripts and the services of the most skillful artisans. It was for the purpose of reaching India by sea to break the Venetian stranglehold on spices that Vasco da Gama and Columbus set forth on their historic voyages. The desire to be first or to possess the unique was just as strong with the Beautiful People of the Roman Empire as it is with the B.P. of New York or Paris. Nero had his equivalent of Camp David in his Golden House, which had a revolving dining-room ceiling that showered rose petals on the assembled dinner guests.

Throughout the Middle Ages the ruling courts and the Church constituted the only buyers for luxury goods. It was not until the seventeenth century, when an affluent merchant class emerged in Venice and Amsterdam, that the royal and ecclesiastical leaders began to have any competition in the marketplace.

The Church was the single greatest patron of artists and artisans; it kept the studios and ateliers busy with its commissions for paintings, sculptures, textiles, wood carvings, illuminated manuscripts, and altar pieces. Money was no object to the court of Pope Urban V at Avignon, where, as Iris Origo wrote in *The Merchant of Prato: Francesco di Marco Datini, 1335–1410,* "The cardinal's mules and horses had golden bits and gold upon their trappings." This was in the fourteenth century, and it was not until the time of the Romanoffs that such lavishness reappeared.

The Marchesa Origo continues:

No less sumptuous—and costing, under John XXII, no less than seven or eight thousand florins a year—were the garments of the papal servants. Twice a year, in spring and autumn, new clothes were distributed to all members of the papal court, while the Pope did not hesitate to buy for his own use forty pieces of cloth of gold from Damascus for the immense sum of 1276 florins. Above all, fabulous sums were spent on furs—even though the use of these was restricted to prelates and members of the papal court. For his personal wardrobe alone, Clement VI used no less than 1080 skins of ermine, while John XXII even trimmed his pillow with them.

The great craftsmen and merchants of the Renaissance were challenged by the same requirements as their counterparts are today. They had to possess a discerning eye for the best, an ability to detect the slightest flaw, and a consuming desire for perfection. They had restricted access to the raw materials of the world, transportation and communications were slow, and markets were small; in compensation they had a readily available force of skilled workmen who had been trained through the apprentice system. The quality-makers and dealers of today must possess identical critical faculties and objectives; all of the great ones I have known had them.

The Industrial Revolution, stimulated by James Watt's improvement of the steam engine in the latter half of the eighteenth century, was destined to have profound effects, but it is doubtful if even the wisest minds foresaw all of the implications which would eventually affect the politics, economics, and social institutions of the entire world. The development of machines, powered by steam, and later by electricity, predestined that hand production would eventually become an anachronism.

The making of things by hand had always involved a personalized, one-to-one relationship, buyer to seller. If the customer wanted an article made in a certain way, whether a buggy or a greatcoat, the artisan had no difficulty in meeting the requirements within the limitations of his own ability. A cabinetmaker or dressmaker might have a model or two to show the patron, but since the article was going to be made to measure, changes were easily incorporated. I can readily imagine a queen telling her dressmaker to lower the neckline to make it more revealing or to make the skirt fuller to disguise her thighs, thus influencing the fashion for her whole court; or a cardinal criticizing the ornateness of a papal casket, and thereby encouraging the artisan toward design simplification. Through the interchange of ideas between discriminating customers and technically skilled craftsmen, elegance was born.

Limited numbers of elegant articles were once produced by man's hand and mind working in concert. The machine that replaced them has a different objective: to make as large a quantity of a single product as the market can absorb, sacrificing, if necessary, some of the subtleties of finish, construction, and color. It does a wonderful job, with the result that more people are able to buy more things at better value than at any other time in history. But few of them are elegant. The machine is capable of making finer articles—provided that the operator has both the intelligence and economic incentive to do so—examples of which I have seen. By the time, though, that the machine is slowed down to produce elegant things, the costs rise almost to that of hand labor. It would be erroneous to conclude that the machine can't be used to produce quality superior to that heretofore achieved. The human mind which invented the machine is also capable of using it to improve its product.

There is a man in Milan who does just that. He is Giovanni Fontana of the Valextra factory, maker of the finest and most expensive leather goods and luggage in the world, to whom even Dr. Gucci tips his hat in admiration. As he took me through his factory, he pointed out certain machines he had invented and built to reproduce the techniques of hand labor. He showed samples of the handmade product and exact duplicates made by the machine. I was unable to distinguish the difference. He uses his machines with great understanding; he does not grind out endless numbers, but he produces limited quantities which satisfy even his standards of perfection. What he has accomplished by an intelligent utilization of the machine, others, also, can do. His merchandise is a rare example of contemporary elegance.

Let us make no mistake about it, elegance was produced at a horrible price: that of human misery. Slave labor made it possible in some periods; paid labor, relatively cheap and abundant, made it possible in others. Eyesight was sacrificed in the making of laces and embroideries. The so-called "blind stitch," a favorite of the Chinese court, was so fine that many of the twelve-year-old-girl embroiderers impaired their sight. A royal court decree later banned such work. Thus, this is no lament for the death of elegance but, rather, a brief retrospective look at what it was and why, and the nature of the strength and weaknesses of the contributions which its successor, the machine, has made to society.

The political and economic conditions which made elegance possible were not consistent with the nineteenth century's democratic concept of government. From the beginning of civilization, man has been making tools of increasing sophistication, including a wide variety of hand-operated machines that were in use in the middle of the nineteenth century. The invention of the steam engine brought mechanical horsepower as a source of energy to the machines heretofore operated by manpower. What is commonly called the "machine age" is a misnomer; it should be relabeled the "power-machine age."

Without powered machines the world's population could not have been supported with clothing, shelter, or food, nor could democratic forms of government have been sustained. Slavery in one form or another would still be in existence. The use of the machine in a competitive economy has made it possible to provide fantastic quantities of goods and superb values to the consumer; the loss of the ultimate in quality is not too high a price to have paid for this achievement.

Understandably, the first impulse in the new age was to use the machine to produce the same goods which had been made previously by hand, but this didn't work out as anticipated. The machine wasn't as good as the hand for carving baroque designs in wood or reproducing the delicate laces or the hand-wrought silver or the leather tooling. Unhappily, it took about a half a century for this idea to be perceived, and for manufacturers and designers to realize that there were many things the machine could do better than the hand if it was fed designs within its capacities. Very simply, this was the rationale behind the development of contemporary design in architecture and furniture. The placement of a carved cornice on a four-story building had visibility to the viewer in the street, but it made no sense at all when located on a forty-story office tower.

The public fought design simplification, but as its eye became accustomed to new forms, it began to accept modern architecture in commercial buildings, although it still held on to traditional Georgian and French designs for homes. More and more the battle for twentieth-century design is making headway and by the twenty-first century it should be won; for not only will the absurdity of reproducing the intricate designs of earlier centuries be apparent to all but the costs of doing so will be prohibitive.

Even with elegance gone, the machine had the potential to provide a variety of grades of quality, and there still remained a continuing demand for the best of what was produced. But the shift from a handcraft to a machine economy brought with it a host of problems, many of which, a hundred years later, are still unresolved.

Machine production removed the buyer from any contact with the maker and inserted several layers of distribution between them, the wholesaler and the retailer. If the buyer needed a variation from the standard model, he spoke to the retailer, who in turn talked to the wholesaler, who eventually transmitted the information to the factory. If the factory was in a highly competitive industry, it was undoubtedly more responsive to special requests than if it was in a monopoly position. What changes were economically possible also depended on the degree of mechanization in a factory. A glassmaker couldn't stop the production line to make six mason jars two inches taller than his standard models, but a dress manufacturer could make a dress two inches longer to meet the needs of an unusually tall woman because his production was a mixture of machine and hand labor.

Since the mass-apparel producer was out of contact with the customer's specific demands, he had to work out average sizes in suits, dresses, and shoes which he thought would satisfy the majority. In the United States, particularly, this has led to a sophisticated apparel-size system with sufficient gradations to assure an adequate fit for anyone not misshapen or abnormally small or tall.

The prime benefits of mass production come from maximum standardization, but since people aren't all alike, compromises have had to be made between ultimate profitability and consumer satisfaction. Better values in automobiles could be achieved if the car manufacturers could concentrate on one model; but since one model wouldn't satisfy all buyers, the makers produce a half-dozen frames and body styles, and achieve variety through interchangeable parts which, together with color and upholstery options, give the buyers a great many choices. The end product is a tremendous value, but elegant it is not.

The establishment of the minimum wage, inflation, and the elimination of the apprentice system have all but eliminated hand production in the needle trades. Since World War II, rising costs have decimated the numbers of custom tailors and shoemakers. Even the French couture, the last bastion of made-to-order dressmaking, has shifted emphasis from that phase of its operations in favor of *prêt-à-porter* collections. Those few which continue custom-made operations do so to give prestige support to their perfume and product-licensing divisions. Semiannual couture showings buy millions of dollars of free publicity for an investment of $500,000 a collection.

The Industrial Revolution didn't have a vast impact on the apparel industries until the 1930s, when rayon was introduced. Ready-made, factory-produced clothes for men and women came into the markets in quantity shortly after the turn of the century, following the popularization of Singer's sewing machine. For the first time rayon provided the garment industry with an abundant supply of low-cost fiber, other than cotton, to use in apparel manufacturing, enabling it to take full advantage of mass-producing, electrically powered machinery. These developments improved the quality and value of low- and medium-priced products, but they had serious and negative effects on the production and sale of fine-quality merchandise. Over the past forty years, quality in many fields of manufacturing has deteriorated, slowly but inexorably. It would be fair to generalize that those products affected by modern technology, such as fragrances, cameras, eyeglasses, electric appliances, radios, and television sets, to name but a few, are better than they ever were, and that those in which handwork was an important factor are poorer than they were.

With the adoption of bigness as a national goal, fine-quality manufacturers and retailers felt the pressure to join the parade. Not only were they concerned with retention of their relative position in expanding competitive markets but rising costs of operation required greater sales volume. They discovered, however, that larger plants and stores did not necessarily result in larger sales, so lower price lines were introduced to attract more customers. In some cases, this process was done skillfully, without damage to the better lines, but Gresham's law, which originally was conceived to describe the activities of money, may also be applied to merchandise: cheap goods drive out fine goods.

From the vantage point of a hill, it's easy to discern the forest. When you're in the valley, you don't see the forest— only the trees. Unfortunately, too many retailers never get out of the valley to be able to view their businesses objectively. In a store, for example, if a lower price range is introduced in a newly created department directed to an age level or to a particular life-style, it's possible to add a new increment of business without dissatisfying any of the existing customers. However, if lower prices or quality are brought into a section with a quality-oriented clientele, the change is immediately visible and resented. The reaction is akin to discovering that your favorite breakfast food has been adulterated with sawdust. For many years, fine stores have successfully operated departments with moderate price ranges under the same roof with their deluxe divisions, just as many airlines carry economy and first-class passengers on the same plane. In stores, the trick lies in the skill with which the mix is handled.

Customers of fine-quality merchandise are very sensitive about the prestige of the store label they wear; the minute they think that the label has become tarnished is the time of defection. Tiffany provides an excellent example of a successful development of a new area of business, which it accomplished with honor and distinction.

Tiffany wanted to bring new, younger customers into its stores for less expensive merchandise without endangering its well-established precious-gem and gold business, so it took advantage of a fashion trend for sterling silver and opened a special section devoted to the silver jewelry designed by the talented Elsa Peretti. The designs were original, imaginative, and wearable, so the young buyers came into Tiffany's, many for the first time, to buy a piece of silver jewelry, packed in a Tiffany box, at prices ranging from $35 to $600. Tiffany developed great additional volume and suffered no loss in prestige, for it had not departed from its traditional standards of good design and high quality.

Many stores faced with the same problem might have decided to add a line of lighter-weight, less expensive fourteen-karat-gold jewelry; this would have been debasement, certain to be resented by the clientele. The terms "fourteen karat" and "sterling" are deceptive, for while they describe the metal content of an object, they do not define relative thickness of the metal. A pin may be correctly labeled as fourteen-karat gold, but the metal may be paper-thin and consequently a third of the price of the identical design made of a thicker piece of fourteen-karat gold. Obviously, the heavier piece will be less subject to dents and distortion.

This point was brought home to me a number of years ago when Neiman-Marcus advertised a sterling-silver telephone dialer in *The New Yorker*. Shortly after the ad appeared, I received a note from Walter Hoving, the chairman of Tiffany, in which he wrote: "Your company should be ashamed of selling such a poor piece of merchandise. Even though it can be labeled in truth as 'sterling,' the metal is so thin it had to be filled with plaster to give it any weight." When I showed our buyer the letter and the cut-through section of the dialer which Mr. Hoving had enclosed, she was defensive. "It's only five ninety-five, what more can you expect? And besides, we've received over a thousand orders." "That makes it even worse," I replied. "Cancel the orders, withdraw the item from your stocks, and don't ever try to justify a poor piece of merchandise on the grounds of price." From then on, we redoubled our efforts to check the weight of all articles made of precious or semiprecious metals. I was grateful to Mr. Hoving for his constructive criticism.

John Ruskin wrote: "Quality is never an accident; it is always the result of intelligent effort. It is the will to produce

The Death of Elegance

11

a superior thing." Fine-quality manufacturers, workers, and merchants understand that good things don't happen by accident; they are made to happen by an unwillingness to accept second best. I helped raise the standards of the Neiman-Marcus buyers by making regular inspections of their merchandise in stock. Invariably, I would single out a necktie with a misprint or put my hand in a coat pocket with a hole in it or find a dress with a missing button. The buyers would remark how uncanny it was that I always discovered the defective piece of merchandise. It wasn't uncanny at all; I was just more observant than they were and had less tolerance for mediocrity. In my wanderings in search for the best, the only things I have found which might disprove Ruskin's thesis are some products of nature, like seashells, feathers of exotic birds, butterflies, mineral specimens. Other natural products, like the hair of the Kashmir goat, the ibex, camel, and vicuña, do require the intelligent skill of weavers to make them into beautiful and luxurious cloths.

Bigness in itself is a destructive influence on high-quality operations, because it not only diminishes the personal involvement of top management in many vital areas but brings with it other distractions that are an even greater threat. Bigger businesses entail bigger problems in finance, labor relations, building programs, employee training, executive development. The ultimate solution often leads in the direction of public ownership, either through the marketing of capital stock or merger. The moment an entrepreneur of fine quality takes in one outside partner or three thousand stockholders, the quality of his business can be affected, for the shareholders invest for three reasons only: security, dividends, and growth. They are notoriously unsentimental about their investments; they are not interested in the architectural style of the factories or the cleanliness of the lavatories—they want increased dividends and higher market prices, and they are perfectly willing for the operating standards of the business to be bent in favor of their own priorities. No longer is the entrepreneur the complete master of his business; to meet the demands of his stockholders, he starts making compromises with his traditional quality. His new status as a publicly held company may force him to become more efficient, which is one of the pluses of having outside stockholders, but when he starts to depreciate the quality of his product by the elimination of two of the ten coats of lacquer on a chair or the pinking of the seams of a dress, or by the substitution of plastic for freshwater-pearl buttons on a sportshirt, he defaults in his position as a quality-maker.

The size of a quality business can range from a single artisan with a helper to one with several thousand employees. The acid tests are whether the boss or his trained associates can maintain the same high standards that made for its success, and whether the devotion to the concept of the best is as strong as it was at the beginning. The independent entrepreneur, whether an artisan or manufacturer, with an idea for a superior product or service, devotes his entire energy to making it the finest available. He has pride in his business and the satisfaction of his clientele. As the sole owner of his enterprise, he is answerable to himself alone, and if the cost of raw materials advances one year, he can make the decision to absorb the price increase or to pass it along. Since he knows most of his customers, he is inclined more often than not to hold the line on price; with his name on the product, the idea of substituting a lower grade is repugnant. Because it is his own money, he can afford to make the decision that it is better business to lose a dollar than to lose a customer.

I have observed that when you talk with an independent fine-quality maker, he speaks with pride about his product; when you talk with the chairman of a large corporation, he refers with pride to its net profit and balance sheet. Be it large or small, every business has to live by the same economic facts of life: they must each be profitable or they will be in financial trouble. The difference lies in attitude. The independent may be so committed to the production of a certain standard of quality that he may be willing to settle for a lesser net profit, temporarily at least. The ultra-big company may have lofty ambitions to maintain the quality of a product from a business it has acquired, but the profit pressures may be so great that it is forced to retreat from its ability to finance its expansion on the most advantageous terms, its opportunity to make new acquisitions, and, finally, dear to the hearts of the executive officers, the value of management's stock options.

Ascribing the most sincere and honest intentions to the ultra-bigs, there is less likelihood that they will maintain standards of fine quality as consistently as the independent owner. The production of the fine and beautiful is not necessarily efficient, and in the attempts to pare costs, the product is very often injured. When the independent quality-maker decides he wants to go public, he will doubtlessly find that the price he has paid is considerably larger than what it first appeared. He will discover that public ownership carries with it not only the wishes of his stockholders but the pressures from the investment analysts who have their own ideas of what his company needs.

In its September 1, 1977, issue *Forbes* magazine reported a case study of a medium-size drug chain which went public and expanded from 60 stores to 650. During their rapid growth they had taken on a lot of debt to be serviced, which led them to make some bad business judgments. The chairman of the company was quoted as saying: "We had constant telephone calls from analysts with suggestions and recommendations which led us to strive for earnings perhaps too rapidly, and to do *things* that were not the healthiest things for the company. . . ."

Dick Salomon, formerly chairman of Lanvin–Charles of the Ritz, wrote a candid article in the *Harvard Business Review*, "Second Thoughts on Going Public," in which he stated:

The average shareholder . . . wants only one thing—to see the price rise. If company action gains that desired effect over a short term, even at the expense of its health, the outsider cheers. If, though, the management looks to the long-range good, he's unhappy.

At the time I was weighing my major decision . . . I should have asked myself certain questions. What I should have asked was: 1. Would I, once I had taken the public in as shareholder-partner, be able to resist or disregard their preoccupation with short-term results and/or fluctuations in the price of our shares? 2. Am I the type who can ignore the stock market demand for consistent and constant increases in sales earnings? . . .

Had I asked myself these questions and had I searched my-self for honest answers, I would have come out with a different solution to my personal problems. I would have held on to my business until such time as I no longer wanted to work in it.

The absorption of small businesses into large, publicly held companies has also resulted in the replacement of "proprietor ownership" by "professional managers," men who have been educated to run anything from a bottling plant to a shoe factory, from a department-store basement to a book-store chain. They know the principles of good management and capital enhancement without having any specialized knowledge of an industry. They do well in high-volume opera-tions, which make the best use of their skills; but the qualita-tive aspects of a fine business suffer under this type of direc-tion—for quality comes about as the result of the experience of an expert who has an intimate understanding of the thou-sand details involved in its achievement. There is an old Spanish proverb which expresses this idea succinctly: *"El ojo del amo engorda el caballo,"* or "The eye of the owner fattens the horse." It's difficult for the professional manager to de-velop the eye of an owner, for he doesn't have a horse.

There may be examples of professional managers who actually founded fine-quality businesses, but, if there are, I am unaware of them. Essentially, they are caretakers and accumulators, capable of expanding established companies and improving their operating statements and P/E ratios, of adding by acquisition. Nowhere is quality more closely related to owner-management than in the restaurant business. In the month of March, a few years back, I was dining for the first time at Le Lavandou, a restaurant on East Sixty-first Street in New York, and ordered melon for dessert. I remem-ber the month, for it occurred to me that anyone ordering melon in March had no right to complain if it wasn't good. The *patron* walked through the dining room attired in his chef's hat and apron, speaking to the guests he knew and smiling at those he didn't. My melon arrived, and though nice in appearance, it was hard. I was able to dig out one spoonful and I quit. When the waiter came back to clear the table, I made no complaint, for, after all, it was March. In a few minutes the waiter returned with another slice of melon and said, "The chef thinks this might please you better." The owner-chef, seeing the piece of melon minus one spoonful, found out what was wrong, and on his own volition replaced it. That's a quality peculiar to proprietorship.

The subtleties of fine-food preparation and service suffer from bigness and the absence of the all-seeing eye of the proprietor. Trader Vic's was one of the great American restaurants when it had a single location in Oakland, and it even survived the installation of a San Francisco branch. Then Vic Bergeron, the founder, succumbed to the lure of establishing Trader Vic's restaurants in hotels all over the country.

Vic had created a unique menu of foods and drinks with recipes of reputed Polynesian origin and with a stage-setting South Seas decor. Despite the fact that Vic had never been west of San Francisco, his research was so good that everything came off with apparent authenticity, at least to the eyes and tastes of most of his customers who hadn't visited Pago Pago themselves.

One night I dined at the Trader Vic's restaurant in the Plaza Hotel in New York where I ordered my favorite Trader Vic dish, Indonesian lamb, which is served with a generous portion of viscous peanut-butter sauce blended, I've always suspected, with soy and mustard. On this particular evening, there was only a small, firm ball of the peanut butter, tightly packed from a number-four ice-cream scooper and placed in a small pleated-paper cup. The consistency was stiff and the extra ingredients had been skimped on. It was obvious an efficiency expert had reduced both the size of the portion and the ingredients in its recipe.

Trader was probably one of the first restaurateurs to introduce the Japanese *oshibori*, the steamed towelettes, to wipe both fingers and lips. Our waiter brought them, after removing our plates, and said "Hot towels." They were damp and cool. I complained, but the waiter had done his job by announcing that they were hot. Whether they were hot or cold was a matter of no concern to him or the captain who stood nearby.

Trader Vic's was noted for pioneering the sale of good

American wines in California, but in New York there was no wine list, and wine by the glass was available only under duress. The final indignity to Vic's great restaurant tradition was when the waiter placed the water pitcher on the head of one of the large wooden Tikis, a decorative element in Vic's carefully conceived design scheme. Out of respect to Vic, and the god the Tiki represented, I asked the captain to remove it, but a few minutes later the waiter replaced it and the captain made no protest. The staff, doubtlessly, had been trained according to carefully planned service manuals, but unfortunately Vic had not foreseen that a waiter might use the head of a Tiki as a service station. This gaucherie may have gone unobserved by most of the diners; many who saw it probably paid no attention, but any institution catering to customers who want the best and are willing to pay the price for it must be concerned with its ability to satisfy the minority. They are the ones who know the difference; they are the ones that the majority will follow.

The market for the best always was worldwide and it is even more competitive today. At fur and jewelry auctions, the successful bidder may be from Belgium, Germany, Japan, or Saudi Arabia, as well as the United States. It has been my experience that as soon as people get money, it doesn't take long for them to seek a higher standard of living, including homes, cars, clothing, and all of the luxuries of life. Television and motion pictures have made the attributes of wealth highly visible and have fed the demand of a growing affluent society.

Although increased taxation and the disappearance of the money-spending nobility have eliminated some purchasing power for the best, such a wide redistribution of wealth has taken place in this century that there are actually more people able to buy the best than ever before in history. True, there is no Czar to support a Fabergé, fabulous maker of gold and jeweled trinkets, nor to commandeer the entire catch of Barguzin sables, but there are scores of buyers of Fabergé *objets* whenever they come up at auctions, and there are several thousand women all over the world who can afford to buy Barguzin sables.

The U.S. Bureau of the Census report of 1980 shows that

not only are there more families with incomes to buy better but there are more that can buy best. Despite higher taxation, there are even more millionaires. The total number of families with incomes over $25,000 rose from 1,460,000 in 1955 to 23,711,000 in 1980. Compared with 1955, the 1980 figure shows a 1500 percent gain.

In *Across the Board,* a publication of The Conference Board, Fabian Linden comments on these statistics:

For marketers, the most significant shifts have taken place at the top of the income scale. Currently the income "elite"—the 20 percent of all families with the highest annual earnings—includes eleven million homes. The minimum income of families in this class is about $22,000; the average income is roughly $30,000. Anyway, this top fifth of the population accounts for more than 40 percent of total consumer spending power.

He then makes another pertinent observation:

One of the more important changes in the characteristics of the affluent is a marked rise in the proportion of families with two or more members drawing a paycheck. An extraordinary 77 percent of our upper-income families have at least two persons in the labor force, while only 22 percent have a single earner—ten years ago that ratio was 30 percent, and twenty years ago it was 35 percent.

This evidence of a dramatic growth in affluence of a large segment of our population suggests that there should be an increasing demand for the best available. I believe this to be true, but I also know that buyers are discouraged by what they perceive to be a deterioration in the quality of both goods and services. Almost daily, customers ask me: "What's happened to quality?" I can only reply with candor, "It has declined."

It is easy to put the blame on inflation, and although that has been an important contributing factor, there are others as well. Rapid personnel turnover at the buyer level has forced the promotion to buying responsibilities of many who are too inexperienced to know how to buy expertly. Unfortunately, many of their merchandising supervisors are equally green and aren't able to offer much critical assistance. There are relatively few buyers in the fashion market today who are considered to be genuine pros, and, sad to say, there are few old-time buyers left who can teach them. In most cases their bosses can't, because their only standards are the profit-and-loss statements.

Some critics ascribe the decline of quality to a lack of its being appreciated by the younger customers, but before we can accept that explanation as fact we should examine the evidence more carefully. Perhaps the demand for casualness was incorrectly interpreted by the stores as desire for junk. Perhaps the stores aided and abetted deterioration by their flight from standards and thereby gave their customers no choice. The deterioration of merchandise quality is foremost in customers' minds—I know from firsthand experience, for I am hit with that question following every lecture I give.

This is substantiated by a study conducted in 1976 by the research organization Yankelovich, Skelly and White, Inc., on the "general public's attitudes toward product quality." The survey showed that 60 percent of those interviewed believed that the quality of products and services had declined over the past twenty years. Even if you discount this figure for those suffering from nostalgia for the good old days, you're still left with a dissatisfied majority, which is convinced that "nothing is as good as it used to be."

The best, in many instances, may not be as good as it used to be, but once manufacturers and retailers realize the size of the market for the best, they will get smart enough to make best better—not elegant, for elegance is dead.

Habit de Plumassier.

A Paris chez N. le Libraire rue St Jacques a la pome d'or.

2

Good, Better, Best

It was a mixed blessing to have a father who had no uncertainty about his taste or standards of quality. As far as Herbert Marcus, Sr., was concerned, the best was none too good and he had unshakable confidence in his own taste. Learning the retail business under his direction was both rewarding and frustrating: he was a difficult man to satisfy, for he always knew how anything could be done better. The standards he set for his home and children were no different than those he had established in his business: he had no tolerance for mediocrity; he expected the best, he got the best. Fortunately, I wasn't cowed by the forcefulness of his dictum but preserved my own ego, even while I absorbed the rigorous indoctrination he gave me. He would have subscribed to the observations of Irma Kurtz in *The Times* (London): "True elegance makes no statement about the bank balance of its creator, but only about his taste." And, "Elegance does not have to be expensive, but even when it is, it must never be seen to be expensive." Although a realist, he was reluctant to admit the demise of elegance.

My education in the subject of quality was later completed by Neiman-Marcus's first buyer, Moira Cullen, a remarkable woman, who gave me experience in the buying field. She trained my eye to see and to search for those things that were the best: the finest methods of merchandise construction, the ultimate in quality, the simplest design. When I completed my five-year-training period under the two of them, I had the equivalent of a Ph.D. in merchandise that no business school could have given me. I learned to differentiate, not between good and bad but between better and best, and to pursue the best, regardless of cost or effort. The difference in cost to achieve the best may be negligible, but overcoming the inertia of the *status quo* and the willingness of most people to settle for less than perfection always takes greater effort.

When buying ready-to-wear in the manufacturer's showroom, it is customary to put an X after a style number if any change is being specified. Miss Cullen was so discerning, so demanding, that almost every style she purchased was X'd. As a result, she was often referred to, behind her back, as "Madame X." Many times I squirmed with impatience as she held up the buying process to criticize the fit of a garment, the quality of the fabric, the design of the buttons, or the shape of the belt. She would call for the designer and point out that the waistline needed to be dropped three-eighths of an inch; she would summon the factory's piece-goods buyer to demand the substitution of a more desirable fabric; she would insist that the findings buyer submit samples of less ornate, but usually more expensive, buttons. It often took as long as a half hour to complete the purchase of a single style, during which time the normal showroom activities were completely disrupted. The manufacturer glowered, the designer fumed, the models grumbled at having to work through a lunch hour, but Miss Cullen was unruffled, and, in her zeal for perfection, continued to rebuild almost every style she bought.

Many buyers are suppressed designers and invoke changes as an ego demonstration; but not so with Miss Cullen, who had no illusions about her designing capability. She was not grandstanding by making her incessant demands; she was simply trying to get as perfect a garment for her customers as possible, and while manufacturers disliked the ordeal of a buying session with her, they invariably followed her requests, having learned from prior experience that she was usually right. Since she rarely had to pay a bonus for her changes, the customer was rewarded with a better product at no extra charge.

Johnny Magnin, when he was head of I. Magnin, was another buyer who liked to make changes. He was another "*X*-er," but his changes mainly had to do with the relocation of pockets on dresses. He was a decisive buyer, except in the location of breast pockets, in which matter he displayed uncertainty as to whether the pockets should be lowered one-half inch or raised one-quarter of an inch, or shifted slightly from one side to the other. He carried on his experimentations in the showrooms while the mannequins endured his pocket "manipulations" with discomfiture.

Miss Cullen was the last of a breed of apparel buyers who knew enough to make constructive changes. The current crop of buyers, recruited from college graduates who have gone through stores' executive-training programs, simply don't have the merchandise knowledge to function in a similar manner. They have been trained to read the computer printouts essential for multiple stores, to balance their stocks by price lines and color, and to latch onto the newest fashion trends, but few of them know or care enough to demand adequate hems, "under pressing," or bound seams.

Today, most stores follow a personnel-promotion program dictated by both their own internal requirements and the pressure of young buyers for quick advancement and new assignments. Too many able trainees are opting for rapid job changes in the mistaken belief that the largest number of job experiences in the shortest period of time is the best qualification for the first management job available. Barely has a shoe buyer learned the difference between calf and kidskin when he is promoted to buy men's clothing. I questioned a newly appointed men's neckwear buyer to ascertain how much he knew about ties, asking the origin of the words "paisley" and "Tremlett," and the significance of a handmade bar tack on a tie. He was unable to answer any of these questions. Of course, this does not prove that he won't eventually be a successful tie buyer, but for at least two years the quality of his neckwear stock may possibly suffer as he learns. By that time he will be moved into another area in which, again, he has no expertise.

Incidentally, the answers to those questions are: "paisley" is the name of a town in Scotland which gained fame for its machine production of Indian Kashmir-type shawls, the de-

*Good,
Better,
Best*

23

signs of which were originally based on the stylized form of the cone or pine (these designs are probably the most popular motif used in men's neckwear); "Tremlett" was the last name of a famous nineteenth-century haberdasher in London who reputedly made the first seven-fold tie from a square of silk, thus eliminating the need for a lining; the handmade bar tack anchors the final fold on the backside of the tie, preventing the tie from unfolding. The machine-made tack holds the fold rigidly; the handmade tack permits a limited movement. Only the finest makers go to the expense of the handmade tack.

Job-hopping eliminates the development of any real understanding of quality, which takes both time and repetitive experiences to achieve. Clinical psychologist Harry Levinson, in an interview with Sam Feinberg of *Women's Wear Daily*, observes: "Moving around to make people eligible for promotion may not be productive. Rapid rotation through jobs may broaden people, but it can also make them shallow. Some jobs require less than two years to be adequately discharged, while others may pay off only with a great deal of intensive effort."

Merchandise deterioration occurs because many buyers don't know what is best, much less where to look for it or how to get it. "Market average" replaces best as a standard without management's recognition of the change. Too often, management has its eyes focused on the comparison with the previous year's profits, not on the quality barometer.

However, in fairness to this generation of buyers, market conditions have changed radically since Miss Cullen's time. Manufacturers have become more inflexible as they have grown larger and are less willing to make changes; fabrics are more standardized, and cost pressures have become greater. Smaller domestic makers and the foreign markets provide the only opportunities for the buyer to exercise quality improvement.

In the field of apparel manufacturing, the actual labor is performed by outside contractors; the manufacturer contributes design, selling, and delivery functions and has limited control on the quality of the merchandise produced under his name. If he is dissatisfied with the quality, he can change contractors. The contractors, being profit-motivated, also try to squeeze the maximum number of garments out of the yardage allocated to them. They may cheat by skimping the seams and shortening the hems, and it is a practice among some of them to "shrink the marker." In this process, the paper marker (on which the component parts of the cardboard pattern are traced) is wadded into a ball, smoothed out, and is consequently shrunk by 5 percent. This may save the contractor one yard out of twenty, which he either sells or makes up into garments for his own account. In past years, when a manufacturer produced his own garments, he knew what was going on in his own factory and could insist on the maintenance of his quality standards. He could also respond more affirmatively to his customers' demands.

The drop in apparel quality should not be blamed entirely on the contracting system alone, for many manufacturers do their own kind of cheating. After they have approved the designs and taken orders from their store customers, they call in their production managers, or "take-out" men, as I call them, to determine what they can take out of the garments by the simplification of the design, or by the substitution of a less expensive fabric for the original, or by the elimination of a skirt lining. If the garment still proves to be too expensive to make, it is simply withdrawn from the line and the buyers are notified that it won't be made because of late fabric delivery. Not all makers follow these practices, but the next time you experience or hear of a skimpy garment, you will know the reason why.

The unions must bear a share of the responsibility for the decline in quality, for they have been concerned more with lifting average wages than in rewarding the exceptionally talented workers. By doing so, they are satisfying the majority of their constituents, but quality suffers as a result.

With few exceptions, retailers do little to examine the goods that come into their stocks. Only a few have inspection departments to check on fit and construction, leaving it to their salespeople or customers to discover any defective merchandise. Large stores usually receive merchandise at a remotely located warehouse which the buyers visit only at infrequent intervals, so it is not easy for them to examine their receipts to determine if the goods were received as bought, if the fabric is the same as originally shown or if there was a substitution, or if the shipment comes up to the maker's normal standards.

A formal inspection system, conducted by trained technicians, in which merchandise is spot-checked at the time of arrival or at the factory before delivery, is an expensive process but the only way that large organizations can exercise any quality control over what they sell. Otherwise they merely give lip service to quality.

One of the most serious efforts to maintain quality standards is that originated by the London retail chain Marks & Spencer immediately after World War II. It recognized that British manufacturers lacked the sophistication to make lingerie and blouses able to compete against the finesse and styling of European production, so it set up a design studio with a staff of competent designers, many of whom were Austrian and German refugees, and backed them with a group of textile engineers. After the designers produced their sample garments, the technicians established fabric and manufacturing specifications with cost estimates for each step in the production process. These, together with the patterns, were taken to the makers, who were told what the garments should cost, including a fair profit allowance. If the cutter demurred and said that he couldn't produce at the given price, the engineers came into his factory and showed him how they could do it. Marks & Spencer was insistent that its suppliers make a profit but, equally, it was adamant that the standards be maintained.

It still follows this procedure whenever the markets require such design assistance, but carries its quality-maintenance program a step further by sending its engineers into the mills and factories to inspect merchandise during the production process. When the mill ships 200,000 yards of fabric to the cutter, and when the latter delivers his weekly order for 12,000 pairs of pants or 50,000 panties directly to the 476 Marks & Spencer stores, the quality of the cloth, the fit and accuracy of sizing of the garments have already been approved. The result is the cleanest and best-made apparel merchandise for the money produced anywhere in the world.

The best in this instance does not imply the finest: it does mean that by great dedication to standards, Marks & Spencer has succeeded in procuring products superior in value to any competitive merchandise. To my knowledge, there is no comparable effort at quality-control in either European or American markets. As a result, it was able to market the best slips, gowns, panties, and brassieres in the English market—facts which were quickly observed by even the most affluent women in London, who might go to Dior in Paris for their gowns, but came home to Marks & Spencer for their lingerie and bras.

Is the best measurable? If so, by what kind of instrumentation? Certainly not by an "applauseometer," as used to record the volume of applause on the "Major Bowes Amateur Night Talent" shows during the heyday of radio. I know of no universal empirical devices, but I do believe that the best is discernible to the observant eye. Sometimes recognition comes slowly, but eventually the discriminating customer discovers the best and passes the word around. The magazines are full of advertisements proclaiming that their products are the BEST, the highest accolade they can bestow upon themselves; but it is the *customer* who finally makes this decision.

Professional buyers in numerous trades employ the comparison method to determine grade, size, and color. It is the one used by fur graders, who sort out bundles of skins by color, texture, and hair-height. They keep on comparing one pelt to another until they have bundled together the number of matched skins needed for a coat. Basically, this is the system used for grading pearls or diamonds, although the criteria differ.

I made it a practice to capitalize on my acquaintanceship with top manufacturers by requesting that they share their knowledge with me, and I was never turned down. Once I went to the foremost neckwearmaker and took with me a half dozen neckties, all in the same relative price range. I laid them before him and asked him to criticize them for me. He examined the unlabeled ties and very quickly pointed out the techniques by which yardage had been skimped in three out of the six.

One tie was shorter than the others by two inches, which

saved an eighth of a yard on a dozen ties; another was made with a tipped lining (meaning that the lining extended only three inches); all three ties had inadequate facings on the final fold, saving another tenth of a yard. Two of the six were made with linings that came to the edge of the tie, instead of being inset in a frame made by the tie fabric itself. Five of the six either had no bar tack or had one made with a flimsy, short machine stitch.

He explained that the .cost of his tie silks varied from $8.00 to $12.50 per yard of twenty-eight-inch-wide fabric. If he used four and one-half yards per dozen ties, he would have an average of $45 in material content alone. If a competitor could reduce the yardage required by as little as one-quarter yard and make the ties by machine instead of by hand, he would save enough to sell ties of the identical fabric for $10 less per dozen. The trick, of course, is to skimp on the yardage in ways that would not be obvious to the unsophisticated store buyer or even less knowledgeable customers.

With increasing prices of pure silk, many tiemakers have resorted to the substitution of light-weight silk and have compensated for this loss of weight by the use of a heavier and stiffer interlining material to give the ties additional body. The customer is not apt to notice the difference until he has worn the tie and finds the stiffness objectionable and the creases in the knot permanent. The objective of the finest makers is to manufacture a tie that is resilient, that will hold together for its life, and that will tie easily with the "dimple" centered under the knot.

Manufacturers in other fields will respond readily if approached by a young buyer eager to add to his fund of knowledge. The only caveat is to select a maker who is the best in his field and who has a reputation for honesty. Usually, *best* makers have that quality, for "best" and "honesty" are clearly interrelated.

An important point, which frequently is not understood by customers, comes out of the tie analysis. Theoretically, any given fabric in a shirt or a suit or a dress can be manufactured in apparently identical models to retail at two or more different prices. The difference lies in the quality of the workmanship and the amount of fabric used in each garment. The same look can be achieved; but one dress may have two pleats instead of four, one shirt may have plastic instead of fresh-water-pearl buttons, one suit may have one inside coat pocket instead of three. One garment may feel skimpy, another roomy and comfortable; the collar of one may stand away from the neck instead of hugging it. One may be machine-made, the others may have sufficient unseen hand labor in the inside construction to help retain shape after wearing. These are the differences which can make a quality product worth its price if the customer can afford the extra cost. Only the men's clothing industry has a grading system for quality of manufacturing. It ranges from grade 1 to grade 6, the latter being the best.

Most women's fashion and shelter magazines do an excellent job in pointing out quality differences between the similar products in the same price zones. *Consumer Reports* performs technical laboratory tests of mechanical and electrical articles to arrive at a comparative product rating scale, but tends to ignore aesthetic values which are of importance to many buyers.

The retail customer should compare the fabrics and work-manship in garments of varied prices. In a relatively short period of time, any customer can add to his expertise and is then qualified to complain when an article is below stan-dard for its price. If the customer is undiscriminating and accepts that which is offered without complaint, then the re-tailer will be less apt to try to demand a better product from the manufacturer. If the manufacturer doesn't get pressure from the retailers, he is not likely to attempt to improve his product.

I've watched many people in various lines of endeavor striving to attain the best, and I have tried to determine what qualities they had in common. Whether they were baseball pitchers trying for a no-hit game, runners attempting to break a world record, or grape growers intent on producing the finest wine in the world, they all had complete dedication to their goals. They displayed greater knowledge than their competitors; they were willing to put in the extra effort neces-sary to approach perfection; they never settled for second

Good,
Better,
Best

best. They exerted themselves to reach these heights of accomplishment for both financial reward and esteem of their peers or clients, and for their own satisfaction.

Such a leader was C. R. Smith, the guiding force of American Airlines for almost thirty-five years. He recognized that after safety, courtesy and better service were the ingredients to build his airline into a position of national pre-eminence. He was not content simply to write directives on the subject, but he rode the line from coast to coast to preach the gospel, becoming personally acquainted with crew members, ground personnel, and ticket sellers. He observed that a certain percentage of passengers had problems of some sort at the ticket counters, and instead of letting them fume to the point that they were "going to write a letter to the president," he defused them by stationing a special passenger-service agent in front of the counter to give the irate passengers an opportunity to pour forth their wrath. He understood that once the problems were solved, the travelers relaxed and continued their journeys in a state of pleasure rather than in one of indignation, thereby eliminating subsequent word-of-mouth denunciations of American.

(I watched this problem-solving technique and applied it to Neiman-Marcus whenever we had customers lined up waiting for some particular kind of service, such as the gift-wrapping department immediately prior to Christmas. It paid off for us equally well.)

He recognized the fact, ignored by so many business leaders, that each employee of American was more interested in his own future than in the company's, so he established programs designed to improve the capabilities of each individual. He insisted on giving not only pilots the best training possible but mechanics as well, for, as he said, "There's nothing a pilot can do if the plane falls apart in midair." He built the first stewardess-training school to teach not only the intricacies of cabin service but to inculcate a standard of courtesy and graciousness that has never been met or surpassed by any airline. He wanted his stewardesses to come off their trips with the feeling of satisfaction of a job well done.

Not only in the school but on his frequent flights, he would tell the flight attendants that they were the best and most important representatives of the company. "I won't order you to be courteous," he would say, "but I want to prove that it is good for you. If you are rough with passengers, it's bad for them, for the company, and for you! It doesn't take more time to be courteous than discourteous, and both the recipient and giver of service and courtesy benefit by having a happier day."

C.R. and I developed a healthy mutual respect and whenever we met, on a plane or in my office, we usually got around to the problems of maintaining the kind of service we both thought was of such great importance to our respective businesses. The last time I saw him, I posed the query as to whether standards of quality and service could survive their founders and, if so, for how long. Could the insistence on the best over a long period act as a semipermanent inoculation for a business? "Sure," he replied, "if you give it booster shots."

If the employees have for so long been accustomed to providing good service that this has become an ingrained habit, a high standard of service will continue for some time after change of management, even if that management proves to be inept. In some organizations, a high standard of service is difficult to eradicate on any immediate basis. On the other hand, a reputation for poor service is hard to overcome. The airline business provides two opposite examples.

In the early days of commercial aviation, when business to Florida was highly profitable, before the jet, which popularized island hopping, Rickenbacker and Eastern had a monopoly on the New York–Florida business. It was so easy to sell space to Florida that Eastern began to believe it was doing the customer a favor to take a reservation. Eastern was then one of the most prosperous of the airlines.

For a long time the service on Eastern was so poor that "I hate Eastern" clubs were formed by disgruntled passengers. In varying degrees, the reputation of Eastern for poor service has endured for more than twenty-five years. Subsequent managements have tried to improve the Eastern image, though that has always proved to be difficult. Today, after many years, the image is brightening, due to the leadership of Frank Borman, but it did take a long time.

Good,
Better,
Best

American, on the other hand, has been able to retain a substantial part of its reputation for good service. In many cases, the employees retained their own concept of good service and provided it, because they had been accustomed to rendering it for a long time. It is comforting to realize that good principles, soundly embedded, are not quickly erased.

Perhaps the pithiest tribute to C.R. was one that appeared in *Forbes:* "Cyrus Rowlett Smith made American Airlines the standard of the domestic industry by treating his passengers like royalty and his employees (with whom he sometimes shot crap) like partners. Under Smith's successor, American became just another airline."

I think that C.R. and I would both disagree with the last sentence of the comment, because there are people at American who still remember the lessons he instilled, sometimes with choice profanity, and they are transmitting them to another generation of employees.

As a retail merchant I've had the opportunity to observe those who knew the best, and those who watched those who knew and followed their lead. Quality to many is an approach *to* or a way *of* life. They have learned from either parents or experience to buy the best they can afford, even if it means buying fewer or less frequently. Obviously, everyone cannot buy the finest diamond or fur, but everyone can buy the best he can *afford*. I've discouraged the sale of countless numbers of second-quality mink coats in favor of the top quality of a less expensive fur.

My favorite complaint came from a customer who wrote that her coat purchased seven years previously wouldn't wear out, but that it was now too short. I replied:

Dear Mrs. Carstairs:

We can either shorten your coat to a three-quarter length for twenty-five dollars or we can add a fox border for two hundred dollars. I would recommend the first solution.

Sincerely,
Stanley Marcus

She took my advice and wrote me seven years later that she had just given her coat to a less fortunate neighbor and that she fully subscribed to the doctrine of "buying the best."

In today's polyesterized world, top store management has limited knowledge of the quality of all of the merchandise it sells. Store apparel buyers are purchasing brands or designer-name lines, and most of them are buying "looks" without paying too much attention to construction or fabrics. They are willing to settle for *good* without fighting for *best*, a generalization that would cover most buyers in today's retail world.

At the beginning of department- and specialty-store development, the owners knew enough about the quality of their merchandise to stamp it confidently with their own names as a guarantee of quality and fashion correctness; they were circumspect in their use of manufacturers' labels.

Then, national brands came into vogue in the 1920s and forced their way into department-store stocks, after having assaulted the public with heavy barrages of national advertising. Soon, however, the stores learned that national brands became the targets for price wars, from which the manufacturers were the only ones to profit. When price-maintenance laws were held to be unconstitutional, the decreased profit margins on national brands caused retailers to use them much more selectively and to develop their own private brands.

In 1983, Levi Strauss blue jeans, which had become the single largest apparel sales item for a sixteen-year period, came under attack in a bitter price war. Under the law, manufacturers cannot set retail prices, nor can retailers agree among themselves to maintain prices, so Levi's became a loss leader in the U.S. markets. This is a phenomenon that invariably occurs whenever a national brand name reaches a position of pre-eminence, for there is always a retailer who thinks he can capitalize on the drawing power of a top name at cut prices.

The specialty stores which had resisted national-brand merchandise because of limited markup and widespread distribution fell into the same trap when they began to promote designers' names. Soon, the prestige names of fashion were so entrenched that they became national brands, without bestowing the benefit of very much national advertising. The department stores, in their eagerness to skim off some of the specialty-store trade, started to add designer names, and the designers, seeing no difference in the color of the money, sold to almost any store willing to write an order.

Although the designers do little or no national advertising, they provide what is called "cooperative" money to the retailer for local advertising on a fifty-fifty basis. They also add some glamour in the way of free publicity in the fashion press and gossip columns. In actuality, many of them are playing a sleight-of-hand game by producing several lines at different price levels and by licensing the use of their names to a wide variety of products of diverse nature, running all the way from chocolates to bed sheets. In addition to her couture collection, Mollie Parnis makes a Mollie Parnis boutique line 50 to 60 percent lower in price. Hanae Mori, the Japanese designer, does the same thing. Geoffrey Beene creates a more casual line under the name of Beene Bag. Givenchy exports his French *prêt-à-porter* dresses to his accounts, who also buy knitwear, shoes, scarves, and hosiery produced under licensing agreements in numerous countries. Quality moves down a notch in each of these supplementary collections. The name may be the same, but the quality is not.

In these days when professional managers, with a limited qualitative knowledge of merchandise, are operating stores, it is easier for them to "trade up" by the use of designer names than to go out in the market and improve the quality of their stocks by more sophisticated selectivity. This new breed of managers is self-conscious of its lack of quality and fashion expertise, which it camouflages by going into the designer-name business. These names become its security blankets.

The designers—who can be as egocentric as actors—greedily insist on individual boutiques within the stores to house their goods. The stores, by yielding to these demands, transform themselves from their historic stance of selectors, editing the merchandise content to their own taste, into a collection of name boutiques, each representing the point of view of a particular designer. They achieve immediate sales increases at the cost of setting up long-range problems that eventually have to be solved.

There is nothing sacrosanct about preserving a traditional role; if, by a carefully weighed change in program, a store can serve its customers better and improve its profits, it should do so. To date, the multiboutique concept hasn't answered either of these objectives. Customer satisfaction suffers because it is difficult for the shopper to locate a specific classification of merchandise, and service deteriorates for purely economic reasons—it is impossible to staff the boutiques with an adequate number of salespeople. Increased shoplifting is the only demonstrable result. The shopping experience deteriorates as customers find identical boutiques in competing stores and standardized stocks of merchandise, and this eliminates the reasons to shop in any particular store. Fashion merchandise thus gets reduced to the level of convenience goods as the customer goes to the shop closest at hand. In the long run, the manufacturer suffers, too; for the quality retailers eventually move away from broadly distributed lines.

Since a designer cannot maintain a constant flow of new merchandise, the boutiques are usually sparsely stocked, except at the beginning of the major seasons. Without frequent arrivals of new styles, sales invariably fall off. Two months of the year the customer finds good selections, the other ten months she will see only leftovers and broken size and color ranges. During the regime of Mildred Custin, Bonwit Teller was a prime example of a store that sold out its own identity to the designer-boutique concept. Bonwit's eventually discovered that it was traveling on a one-way street and changed course, but despite the failure of the Bonwit revolution, many other stores didn't learn the lesson and are continuing to succumb to designer pressure. Someday, stores will return to the job of storekeeping, not designer glorification.

When a store had no branches, it was much easier to keep up with customer demand, service, and fashion trends. The boss was there and he could make personal observations of what was going on instead of having to read reports from his

subordinates. He could even get behind the counter to wait on a customer, and in the course of doing so, learn more about his business than the computer printouts tell him today.

The elephantine growth of stores has forced the managements to devote a large portion of their working hours to budgeting and the solution of operational problems; expansion programs demand attention for reviews with the architects and interior planners. The result is that there is an inadequate amount of time left over to devote to the two most important elements of a retail business: merchandise and customers. Under these conditions, it is inevitable that the quality of both goods and services will deteriorate sharply.

As a test, I telephoned twenty retail-executive friends in various cities between nine-thirty and eleven o'clock in the morning. I was able to reach only one person on the first call; the others were in "closed door" meetings. When I did talk to the others subsequently, I asked them to describe the general nature of the meetings. Without exception, the meetings were on the subject of expense control, new store development, or sales budgeting for the next season. Not a single meeting was held on the subject of store service or merchandise quality. I seriously doubt if there has been a merchandise meeting of top executives devoted to the subject of a handbag: how to improve it by making it larger or smaller, by using a better quality of leather or lining, by strengthening the construction for greater longevity, or by sewing it with smaller stitches. True, this responsibility has been delegated down the line to the buyer and the divisional merchandise manager, but when

*Quest for
the Best*

the buyers feel that senior management is not as much interested in merchandise quality as in the sales gain over last year, then they cannot be expected to have a dedication to quality improvement. The missing ingredient in most stores is the enthusiastic encouragement from the boss to attain and improve quality standards of merchandise and service. When the boss gets excited, so does everyone else in a retail organization.

Management listens to customer beefs, and when they hear them frequently enough, they will move to improve quality and to correct abuses. Even General Motors took action, belatedly, when its management was dismayed to find that car buyers were unhappy about its engine interchange policy of putting Chevrolet engines in their Oldsmobile, Pontiac, and Buick models. They finally agreed to make a cash refund or to give extended warranties to guarantee satisfaction. With the highly layered structure of a huge company like General Motors it just took more time for the complaints to get to the top than it would have at Bergdorf Goodman's.

What this country needs today is not more consumer movements, but more customers who squawk; not more Ralph Naders, but disgruntled buyers who take their complaints directly to the top management of stores in which they shop. It's not enough to reject unsatisfactory merchandise or adjustments; the customers must also register the complaints directly with the management officials.

Here is:

A Customer's Bill of Rights

1. The Right to expect polite service—if there is any.
2. The Right not to be intimidated by salespeople.
3. The Right to expect salespeople to know something about the merchandise they are selling.
4. The Right to complain about shoddy, substandard merchandise.
5. The Right to compliment superior quality of service and merchandise.
6. The Right to expect a store to stand behind its merchandise.
7. The Right to accurate and efficient billing, despite the computer.

Good,
Better,
Best

Habit d'Orlogeur.

A Paris, Chez N. de Larmessin, Rue St. Jacq., à la Pomme d'Or.

3

Service Goes Down the Drain

Wartime labor shortages forced many stores to accelerate an already existent trend toward self-service; after the war, minimum wages and other increased costs of doing business made it impossible to return to the previous standards of staffing. But stores were not the only institutions which suffered from a lack of trained personnel as people shifted from one type of work to another, fleeing from poorer paying, less attractive positions to better ones. Consequently, it became difficult to attract workers into domestic service, garbage removal, and dishwashing, until pay scales and improved hours and working conditions became competitive with employment opportunities.

The war caused the greatest human mobility this country had ever experienced as wives moved across the country to be near their husbands in military service. Stores lost not only male employees of military age but their wives as well. They picked up some new employees in this shuffle, but they also had to dig deep into the pool of women who had not worked previously. Good as some of these turned out to be, many lacked the experience and skills of trained salespeople, accustomed to serving the public. Unfortunately, the stores did not then, nor do they now, have sophisticated training programs to teach people how to sell. They do a good job of instruction in the writing of sales checks and delivery forms, but they do very little teaching about the merchandise being sold or the method of closing a sale. Most stores leave it to the customers to train salespeople in the techniques of selling.

A seller's market brings out the worst in human beings, whether they be manufacturers or retailers, machine operators or salespeople. Competition is the bloodstream of a free economy, and once that is curtailed, the system begins to become atrophied. When there are more customers than goods to sell, the manufacturer tends to become arrogant; he assumes the attitude: If you don't want it, I have a dozen other customers who do. He becomes less willing to accommodate special requests for a change in color or fabric or for anything requiring unusual effort. This same attitude pervades a sales force that finds selling too easy; it ceases to regard each and every sale as a challenge to satisfy. I received my retail selling and buying experience during the Depression, when there were more goods than customers, from which I learned the invaluable lesson of making every sale count, and I have never forgotten it.

Goethe summarized it correctly when he wrote, "Nothing is harder to bear than a series of good years." The human being, sadly, is not constituted to accept continuous success; he needs the leavening force of adversity to maintain his equilibrium.

The psychological impact of the war brought about a great change in the work ethos both in the United States and in Europe, and particularly in Great Britain. After the war, the Puritan-inspired ideal of an honest day's work gave way to the questions: "Am I getting my fair share?" and "Why should I bash my brains out? There are plenty of other jobs around." These attitudes, plus the fatigue from the war effort, made many people in the work force less willing to put forth the extra energy needed to do an assignment well. Many were in new jobs and knew nothing of the traditions of the business they were working for and cared less, for they did not regard themselves as long-term employees. This state of mind sapped the spirit of competition and the desire for personal attainment.

Help grew so scarce that it became a standing gag to order a personnel department to "bring people in as long as their bodies are warm." Industry was forced to lower its standards for a period of time, during which the supervisory force became accustomed to impoliteness, surliness, and sloppy performance. Even worse, new people came into supervision who never knew it any other way. I recall checking one of our beauty salons and noticing that the manicurist failed to put warm water in her bowl to soak the customer's hand. I called this to the attention of the store manager, who thanked me, saying, "I've just been having manicures for the past five years and I never knew that they were supposed to change the water between hands. I've always had it cold." It was a case of the blind leading the blind.

In the retail field, as I have mentioned, rapid expansion forced constant movement of people, to the point where few developed any expertise. It became an era which failed to nurture the critical eye, because the eye was focused on short-range profits and not on long-range customer satisfaction. The use of part-time employees became an economic necessity, both to improve staffing at peak hours and to tap a new source of labor supply. In so doing, the objectives were accomplished, but there were inadequate efforts made to find ways to train the short-hour midday and nighttime employees in merchandise knowledge and store traditions of service. The five-day week further contributed to the deterioration. Collectively, all of these forces were responsible for service going down the drain.

Not too much damage is done if a seller's market is of short duration, but we have had such a succession of these conditions during the war and postwar periods that we have a whole generation of people in all types of industry, from the hotel business to retailing, who have never learned the necessity of aggressive selling, the elements of common politeness that include the graciousness of saying, "Thank you."

During the war, and in the years succeeding, I was particularly aware of the dangers of the prosperity our business was enjoying, so I redoubled my efforts to talk personally with members of our staff to warn them of the pitfalls of success. Any business responds to leadership from the top, and if management is willing to make the effort of injecting itself, it can pretty well establish the attitudes it desires. People, I've found, want and respond to inspiration, but that stimulation has to come with some frequency. It's not enough to define the goals once a year: it's necessary, by personal contact, for an organization to know that the boss is aware of what's going on. Service, or the lack of it, doesn't come through on the computer printouts; it has to be observed.

Bigness, of course, is the enemy of quality in service, just as it is in product. When a business enterprise becomes far-flung geographically, management depends on standard operating procedures written out in detail. This is the reason you receive uniform services at Hilton hotels and identical hamburgers at every McDonald's, wherever you may be. They, respectively, have perfected training methods to provide the guest with adequate, but impersonalized, attention and unvarying hamburgers. I don't intend to knock their accomplishments, for they do a better training job than most stores. These giant enterprises operate exactly like mass-manufacturing plants. They produce efficient service or a product at a reasonable price but, because of their size and the remoteness of their management, they can permit no exceptions or deviations from their standardized procedures.

This operational rigidity was demonstrated to me in Atlanta shortly after the opening of a plush hotel complex with its own shopping center and amusement park. Attracted by its newness and the management's warm letter of invitation to stay there, I booked reservations that were duly confirmed. On arrival I registered, after waiting for a few minutes for the receptionist to finish a phone conversation. He studied my registration form and, without looking up, he asked for my American Express or Carte Blanche credit card. I replied that I didn't carry these cards, but would pay by cash. "In that case," he replied, "you will have to pay in advance." I assured him I had no intention of complying with such a request and that I would find another hotel for my overnight visit. I was leaving the lobby when the assistant manager came up and wanted to know what was wrong. I explained that the hotel and I did not see eye to eye on the matter of advance payment, particularly in view of the fact that I had a confirmed reservation. He apologized, saying that the room clerk had misinterpreted the rules, and insisted that I come back and occupy a complimentary suite. I accepted his apology and agreed to stay but declined his generous offer. The room clerk had not misunderstood the hotel's policy, for it had been drilled into him; but the hotel had been mistaken in its belief that such a policy would be acceptable to travelers who had taken the trouble to reserve in advance. The hotel had ample time to check my credit rating prior to my arrival.

As department and specialty stores have expanded with branch operations, they have done a good job of mastering their merchandising problems with the assistance of computers; but because of cost pressures, they have staffed their stores inadequately and they have failed to adopt modern training techniques, already developed by other service industries, to prepare their salespeople to serve their customers satisfactorily. The reason there are so many stores in shopping centers can be attributed in great part to the number of lost sales that each store engenders. They prosper on each other's failures.

Large retailers have a higher turnover rate of employees than smaller ones, partly self-induced by the rapid movement of executive trainees, partly imposed upon them by voluntary departures of employees who choose to move to a more personalized-store environment, and partly caused by staff layoffs that are orchestrated to coincide with lags in business. Whichever the reasons, it is difficult to build an esprit de corps that is prevalent in smaller stores where the owner is available to answer questions which are not written out in the book of standard operating procedures. The owner is apt to fight for each sale even if it involves an immediate long-distance phone call to determine the availability of a special order. He takes a "can do, will do" attitude which becomes contagious to his sales force; whereas, in large stores, both salespeople and supervisors shrink from going through the red tape involved with "specials." The large institution is apt to consider its role as being that of a quartermaster, dispensing what it has in stock on any given day; the smaller store regards itself as a supplier to the needs of the individuals who are its customers.

Customers have learned not to expect service from discount stores, motels, supermarkets, but they feel cheated when they don't receive it from department and specialty stores, hotels, epicure shops. Customers have the perception that service is an indication of interest in them as individuals, not just as robots dispensing money. Service means courtesy, graciousness without obsequiousness, appreciation in the form of recognition of patronage, perhaps just a "thank you," willingness on the part of the seller to go beyond the call of duty on occasion, remembering to telephone when a wanted size or style arrives in stock. All of these qualities add up to the creation of a state of euphoria, which in turn fosters customer loyalty to hotels, stores, automobile dealers, and every other organization which customers patronize.

The very fact that these attributes don't exist in abundance today may be ascribed to the bigness of so many institutions, banks as well as stores, which have gotten a blurred image of the individual in their efforts to focus on the mass markets. I would not want to go so far as to say that large companies are incapable of rendering service, for I think man can do anything, within reason, if he wants to do it badly enough, but to do so, he must put forth considerably more effort than he has in the past.

Specialty-store retailing is a business of minutiae, things which may not be of monetary significance, but of great importance, to the customer. Early in the game I learned to carry a notebook so that I could jot down observations and clues customers dropped by chance. If I overheard a woman mention at a party that she had been unable to find a particular article, I would locate it the next morning and have a salesperson call her to tell her we had found what she was looking for. One night, during intermission at a symphony performance, a man I knew approached me to mention that he had bitten through the stem of the pipe he had bought and had been advised there would be a three-month delay for its replacement. The following day I called the buyer and told him the story. "That's ridiculous," he said. "We have just received a new shipment of stems. The salesman must not have known of their arrival. Give me the customer's name and I'll call him." By the time the man had arrived at his office, there was a message on his desk that Neiman-Marcus was delivering the replacement before noon.

Obviously the customer was flattered and pleased. He

called me to thank me and to say that he didn't realize that service of this type still was in existence. A month later, he came to the store and made a purchase of a $50,000 diamond ring. Perhaps the two incidents had no relationship. I like to think they did.

Good, intelligent selling, like service, has gone into an eclipse in most industries except for the life-insurance industry, which teaches its agents how to sell as well as how to fill out an application. Contrary to popular opinion, customers like to be sold, if, and when, they get in the hands of an authoritative salesperson who knows the stocks and shows an understanding of their needs. I'm not referring to high-pressure selling, for that involves selling something the customer doesn't want or need. Admittedly, customers in a Neiman-Marcus store are apt to have more discretionary income than those in other stores, but every store sells its customers only a small percentage of what they are capable of buying.

I witnessed one of the finest demonstrations of creative selling in the Neiman-Marcus men's store one day by a young buyer, Dean Ferguson, whom I had originally employed a few years previously because he had the temerity to ask if there was any reason he couldn't become president of the company in fifteen years. I told him that it was impossible to make him a promise other than that his ability and performance would be recognized. He became the top furnishings salesman in his first nine months and this feat earned him a promotion to a buyership of men's neckwear. We were visiting one of the out-of-town stores and he was showing me some newly arrived neckties. A saleswoman approached him and asked if he could help her out by writing up a sales check so she could wait on another person. She handed him the $15 tie and introduced him to the lady customer. As he started to write the check, he looked up and said, "This is a beautiful tie you have selected. What is he going to wear it with?" The woman reached into her purse and pulled out a swatch of fabric. Dean looked at it a moment and said, "There's an ancient madder pattern which comes in two color combinations that would go very well with this suit." He pulled out the two ties as he was talking to her. She readily agreed and took both of them—at $22.50 each.

Dean asked, "Doesn't he need some new shirts to go with his new suit?" The customer replied, "I'm glad you asked; he does need some, but I haven't been able to find any white ones with French cuffs. Do you have any size fifteen–thirty-three?" He showed her two qualities, pointing out the difference in the cloths. She selected three of the more expensive shirts at $40 each. "Doesn't he ever wear colored shirts?" Dean inquired. "Yes, if you have this same shirt in blue I'll take two."

I was watching the progress of the sale with great interest, wondering what his next ploy would be, or whether he was going to stop while he was ahead. He didn't disappoint me; he was in command, and the customer obviously liked the professional attention she was receiving. He reached into the case and took out a pair of cuff links to show her. "Here's an interesting new cuff link that a lot of our customers have liked much better than the ones they've been using. They are gold-filled and with this Florentine finish, they won't show any scratch marks. They are fifty dollars," he said as he inserted one of the links into his own cuff. She couldn't resist them, and he added them to the sales check.

"Since you liked the ancient madder ties, you might be interested in a travel robe with a matching ascot that we had made in England out of the same fabric." He took one off the rack and tried it on to show it to best advantage. "It is a hundred and sixty-five dollars including the ascot." "That's great," she said, "I'll give it to him for his birthday." By this time, Dean had already pulled out two $45 pairs of pajamas in colors harmonizing with the robe, and asked if she didn't think the gift would be more complete with them and a pair of $50 Italian soft calf lounging slippers. She took them all, and Dean assured her that the robe, pajamas, and slippers would be specially gift-wrapped in a birthday package and marked for delivery the day before the birthday. The woman was grateful and vowed she would never think of shopping elsewhere in the future.

By this time the original saleswoman was free and Dean turned over a sale of $615 which was built on the $15 tie the saleswoman had sold and was willing to settle for—an increase of 4000 percent. What was of even more importance, he had made a firm new customer for the department. When it was all over, I congratulated him on one of the greatest examples of good selling I'd ever seen but that, being a perfectionist, I had detected one flaw. I asked him why he hadn't sold her socks to go with her husband's new suit. He hit his forehead with his hand in disgust. "That's what I like about working for you. You won't settle for less than a hundred-percent performance. I'll call her this afternoon and ask if she'll let me select a couple of pairs." He did; she acquiesced with pleasure; I was satisfied. He was promoted to an assistant-store-manager position, and before he left to take his new post, he came to see me. "Remember the question I asked when you employed me? Well, I am three years ahead of my schedule!"

Not once in the course of the sale did he make reference to the fact that he was a buyer. Not once did he oversell; he related to the customer's needs and knew the content of the stocks well enough to fulfill her requirements. Above all, he had the heart of a salesman who not only thoroughly enjoys the excitement of meeting the expressed request of the customer but had the imagination to conceive of other things the buyer might find of interest. This type of selling technique can be taught; unfortunately, it is not. Americans have always prided themselves on their selling ability, but the bad lessons learned during the sellers' market and the lack of managements' attention to selling have dulled our skills.

When I was on the promotional tour to launch my book, *Minding the Store,* and autographing books in stores all over the country, I was appalled by the quality of selling I observed and by the lack of knowledge of stock content. Obviously, I was mainly concerned with the sale of my book, but at the same time I am enough of a professional seller to want to take advantage of the traffic. When customers came in to buy an autographed copy of my book, I'd suggest another book they might also find interesting. If they were middle-aged, I'd say: "Have you read Michener's *Centennial,* which has just come out?" Or, if they were college types, I'd recommend Edwin Newman's *Strictly Speaking*. It was amazing to find out how many extra sales I made for the bookstores.

One day as I was autographing I heard a woman ask if the store had a book on how to write poetry. The salesperson replied that they did not stock any book on that subject, and as the customer was about to walk away, I looked up from autographing, and said: "Excuse me, but when I came into the store, I noticed a rhyming dictionary. It's over on that table," and I got up and handed it to her. "That's great, I'll take it," she said. The salesperson rang up a $29.50 sale and didn't even thank me. This occurred in a shop operated by one of the large book chains, which might find they could sell as many books at greater profits if they replaced their untrained staffs with vending machines.

If you know what book you want and if you have the exact title and author's name, then the chains can serve you well. They will be more likely to have stocks on hand of the best-sellers because they buy in large quantities. If you want to browse or to ask questions about a book and expose yourself to a literary treat rather than a buffet of publishers' closeouts or reprints, the independent bookseller will give you more satisfaction.

Since bookstores can return unsold copies of most titles to the publishers for credit, and since stores usually extend the same privilege to their customers, I very quickly came to the conclusion that merely autographing a book did not give assurance that it was a final sale. I decided to take a little more time to inscribe the book with the name of the buyer or recipient, with the result that more copies of my book stayed sold. After all, an author's royalty is figured on net sales after all returns. The buyers were pleased by my willingness to inscribe, the booksellers were happy to know that few copies of *Minding the Store* were going to come back, and I felt the extra effort was well invested.

One of the best sales stories I have ever known about had to do with a man named Chester Judis, who was president of the "Hollanderizing" fur-cleaning division of A. Hollander

& Son, fur dressers and dyers. This company had developed the best fur-cleaning service in the industry and served most of the top furriers, who found that Hollander could handle their cleaning better and at a lower cost than they could in their own shop. Among their most prized accounts was Marshall Field, whose business they had taken care of for many years, against all types of cut-rate competition. Field's would stray once in a while, tempted by lower prices, but they always came back to Hollander, whose quality and reliability more than compensated for any price difference.

One day, Judis learned that Field's new storage manager had decided to divide the business with a competitor. He was positive that payola was involved (the rival cleaner was notorious for getting business in this manner) but there was no way of proving it; he decided he had to go to Chicago to straighten the matter out and to save the account. He told his young assistant, Stanley Katz (now the head of a leading New York advertising agency), to come with him. When he arrived at Field's, he first went to see George Metheral, the fur buyer, who was so straight that he never allowed a manufacturer to even buy him lunch.

He told his problems to Metheral, who threw up his hands, saying: "Storage and cleaning are not my departments. I know your cleaning is the best, but there is nothing I can do." Judis replied: "Oh yes, there is. I want to see the president of the company, and I want you to come with me."

They went up to see the president, who did not know that the cleaning business was being diverted from Hollander, but expressed an interest in the differences between the Hollander method of cleaning and the competitor's. Judis said: "The difference is so great that it's visible fifty feet away, and I'm going to prove it to you." He insisted they all go down to the vaults for a demonstration with the storage manager present. When they arrived at the storage area, Judis said: "I want you to line up four chairs at the end of the room, fifty feet away from the racks," and turning to the storage man, "and I want you to pick out a group of coats cleaned by Hollander and by my competitor. I'll pick out the Hollander-cleaned coats from this distance." As the manager held up a coat Judis would call out, "Hollander, Hollander, competitor, Hollander, competitor, competitor" until they had gone through some hundred garments.

The president was astounded, and said: "If there is so much difference thàt you can identify them at this distance without a single mistake, then we will stick with Hollander." Judis thanked him and took the next plane to New York.

On the way back, Katz turned to Judis and said: "I know our cleaning is better, but how could you tell the difference so far away?"

"It was simple," he explained, "Hollander-cleaned coats are shipped on hangers with longer necks." Six months later the competitor was caught in a bribery case by another retailer and went out of business.

Many large sales present problems and sometimes dilemmas. I have experienced many problems, but maintaining a steadfast standard of a single-price policy has prevented me from getting into many dilemmas. The other rule I've lived by is the principle upheld by my father, who stated: "No sale is a good sale for Neiman-Marcus unless it is a good buy for the customer." These principles have answered both problems and dilemmas.

One day I received a call from one of our saleswomen that a Mrs. Z. Z. Smith (that was not her real name) from Houston would like me to come down to the fitting room to see a dress she was considering. When I entered the fitting room she had on a magnificent $7500 beaded evening gown designed by Adrian, the Hollywood designer.

She opened the conversation by saying: "This is the most beautiful dress I've ever seen, but the price is outrageous."

I agreed with her on both counts and told her: "You are superb in the dress, which looks as though it might have been custom-made for you. When we bought it, I was aghast at the price, too. I complained about it to Adrian, who told me there were two thousand beads sewn on by hand. He asked if I'd be willing to hand-sew that many beads for any amount. He wouldn't budge a penny on the price."

That didn't satisfy her. "You know I've been doing business with you for many years, and this is the first time I've ever asked you to change a price."

"Yes, Mrs. Smith," I replied, "you have been a very faithful customer and you've been shopping with us long enough to know that we have one price and that's the price on the ticket. We have never made special prices and you should be ashamed to even ask me for one."

"Well," she said, "your buyer made a bad purchase in paying so much money for this dress and you're going to have to mark it down, sooner or later. I'm going to Europe tomorrow, and if you mark it down to five thousand dollars I'll take it. No one will ever know about it."

"You may be right that we will have to mark it down," I replied, "but when that time comes, the price will be changed publicly and the first customer who wants it can buy it at the new price."

Still protesting, she took a final shot: "You're making a mistake. No one will ever pay seventy-five hundred dollars for this dress."

"Possibly so," I said, "but we will have to take our chances."

"Are you a sporting man?" she asked. "I'll bet you a hundred dollars that you won't get the seventy-five hundred for it, but if you do you'll have to agree to tell me what damned fool bought it."

By this time I was getting tired of the discussion and felt it was worth $100 to get rid of her, so I said, "You're on."

She went on her way to Europe and I forgot about the matter until a week later when I ran into the sales director of our couture department. "An interesting thing happened this morning," she told me. "A man came on the floor with an attractive young woman and bought her the Adrian dress that you were showing Mrs. Smith." I was delighted with the good news. She added, "He wrote a check for seventy-five hundred dollars, and it was signed by Mr. Z. Z. Smith!"

"Good Lord!" was all that I could reply.

Seven weeks later, Mrs. Smith returned from Europe and stopped over in Dallas on her way back to Houston. She called for me. "Well," she asked, "did I win my bet?"

Here was my dilemma. Should I tell her the truth and take the risk of breaking up a marriage? Or should I tell a white lie? I reached into my pocket, took out my wallet, drew forth a $100 bill, handed it to her, and said, "Mrs. Smith, you had better judgment than our buyer. You were right, we did have to mark the dress down at the time of our clearance."

Remembering the principle that "No sale is a good sale for Neiman-Marcus unless it is a good buy for the customer," I could only hope that Mr. Smith had made a good buy!

Habit de Peintre,

A Paris chez N. de L'Armessin, Rüe St Jacques, à la Pôme d'Or.   Avec. Privil. du Roy.

4

Taste

It is reported that Renoir once said to Cézanne, "How can you wear that cravat? Can't you see it's in bad taste?" To which Cézanne replied, "If it were in bad taste, I wouldn't be wearing it."

This assertion was reflective of Cézanne's egotism or self-confidence, either of which is an essential characteristic of the tastemaker. There are different kinds of taste—taste in food, which is related to the physical senses; taste in manners, which is associated with the mores of the time; and aesthetic taste, which has to do with the selection of objects, colors, proportion of forms, and the harmonious arrangement and use of them. Regardless of which taste we may be talking about, "good" taste has as its prerequisite the elements of discrimination, knowledge, and experience.

At best, taste is a matter of opinion, subject to changing times and fluctuating evaluations. Each person is entitled to his own taste opinions, but some more so than others. There is bad taste, good taste, and superb taste; there is insecure taste and sure taste; there is conservative taste and garish taste. Many tend to overrate the quality of their own taste, and they take great umbrage when it is questioned. Others, who are unsure of their taste, mask their insecurity by purchasing articles with designer labels or "as seen in *Vogue*" tags.

Many a fight has occurred over challenges to another's taste; it is more prudent to accept the philosophically valid

Latin phrase, *de gustibus non est disputandum,* "there is no disputing about taste." And, as the late James Laver, the British fashion historian, wrote in *Taste and Fashion,* "Few of us would be willing to admit without argument that another man's taste is as good as ours." The most melancholy task I have ever performed was to tell a buyer that she had bad taste.

There is wide disagreement as to whether taste is an innate or an acquired characteristic. Some tastemaker designers like James Galanos and Gustav Zumsteg, head of Abraham of Zurich, one of the world's finest textile firms, are convinced that people are born with the trait. Other fashion leaders are fuzzy on the subject, although I think they secretly would like to believe they inherited their talents.

Good taste, I am convinced, can be acquired through environment and education; the eye can be disciplined to differentiate between good and bad by a constant looking process, and any person with a normal IQ can develop good taste. The achievement of superb taste is as difficult as the attainment of perfection in any endeavor.

I find myself in agreement with La Rochefoucauld, who wrote in his *Maxims,* "Good taste is the product of judgment rather than of intellect." Although taste may be a characteristic transmittable by heredity, I don't know enough about genetics to know if this is factually valid. The faculty of judgment is necessarily based on experience, comparison, and discrimination. In fifty years' experience as a retail merchant I've never seen anyone successfully intellectualize a taste decision; I've witnessed thousands of customers and salespersons improve their standards of taste by observation and emulation. As a merchant, I refused to let any article be offered for sale I thought was in "bad" taste, but that doesn't mean that some things didn't get by me and that I didn't make some errors of judgment. The slips were accidental and not for profit.

One such slip took place in our fur department at the time when stenciled furs came into vogue. Some of them were very good, but one day my eye lit on a mink coat which had been imprinted with the design of peacock feathers. Peacock feathers may be good on a peacock, but on mink the effect was garish and horrible. I told the buyer in the most explicit terms that I thought the piece was a disaster and that I never wanted to see it again. He gave me a feeble argument, but I was insistent; he agreed that it would be removed from stock. I didn't give it further thought until about nine months later, when, on a visit to our store in Bal Harbour, Florida, I saw this same coat being fitted on a flashy blonde. I started to intervene, for I didn't want to sell it to anyone. The department manager saw my anguish and explained to me that the young lady was a stripper in a local nightclub, and that the garment fitted in perfectly with a new "peacock" number she was going to do. I acquiesced to the sale on the condition that we receive no credit in the program. The fur buyer had thought that by sending the garment thirteen hundred miles away that I would never see it again!

Until the effects of the Industrial Revolution were felt in the early part of the nineteenth century, taste was the prerogative of the rich, the landed gentry. Mass production called for mass consumption, and so began what Russell Lynes in his book *The Tastemakers* calls the "Age of Public Taste." "Taste," he wrote, "became everybody's business and not just the business of the cultured few." Machines, born of the Industrial Revolution, brought wealth to thousands of machine toolmakers and product manufacturers; they made consumer goods available to the mass public at price ranges which they could afford. Neither the public nor the manufacturing trade which served it had very much taste experience, so the two had to learn together. For the past one hundred and fifty years, there has been a program in progress to elevate public taste but, if anyone thinks the battle has been won, a visit to airport terminals in the United States or Europe and an observation of the apparel worn by the passengers will dispel that idea. If that is not convincing, take a look at the wares being sold in the airport gift shops.

Kitsch, the wonderful German word meaning tacky, or corny, is the only worthy description for the vast majority of products offered to the flying public and, parenthetically, I might note that no nation has a monopoly on the production of kitsch merchandise. The French make as much as any other country, as visitors to Mont-Saint-Michel can testify. For the most part, the goods look as though they were produced as candidates for a forthcoming "Guinness Book of Horrors." The notable exceptions are the products in the airport shops in Paris, Amsterdam, Copenhagen, and Seattle.

In a discussion with an important French fashion leader, I questioned him as to the difference between French and American tastes. He made three basic points:

1. France is a small country and the many people from the provinces who visit the capital are influenced by the Parisian look.
2. The large French catalogue firms do not carry as much weight as your Sears Roebuck, J. C. Penney, or Montgomery Ward.

   The shopkeepers in small towns of 10,000 residents go often to Paris and have great influence on their clientele.

   The large retailers who have branches all over France consequently have greater interest in the industrial workers, who make more money and are much more up-to-date than farmers.

   Consequently, the selection offered by French branch stores and catalogues is more sophisticated than that of their American colleagues.
3. French youth, although quite influenced by the so-called American look, are not quite as eccentric.

   They also wear jeans but like them clean and use nice accessories.

Much as I respect my French colleague, I can't say that I fully agree with his conclusion, for I find French mass taste is not any better than American, if as good.

The spotlight was focused on the subject of taste in the 1920s and 1930s, when museums started to stage "good-taste" exhibitions in an effort to raise the level of public appreciation. They showed examples of articles in good and in bad taste in juxtaposition. In the years 1950–55, the Museum of Modern Art went so far as to sponsor a "good-design collection" in collaboration with the Chicago Merchandise Mart. Later, magazines and newspapers established special sections devoted to "Living," and art became publicized in a manner unequaled in any period of history. This has resulted in record-breaking museum attendance, bringing huge crowds which have taxed museum facilities and security.

Manufacturers and retailers have tried to cash in on this new public interest in art by producing and distributing a vast number of art-related objects of porcelain, silver, pewter, and wood in large "limited editions," sometimes limited only to the number for which orders are received. Gullible neophyte collectors, lured by inveigling advertisements, have bought commemorative silver coins, medals, porcelain birds and animals, and reproductions of the Egyptian treasures in the expectancy that they were purchasing objects which would rise fivefold in value in years to come. If I read the future correctly, they are destined to disappointment in many of their acquisitions, which will do well to sustain even the original cost.

The public taste still is far from being sure, so advertisers of filing equipment, dishwashers, and window blinds advertise their products as being in "decorator colors" to give proof positive that the colors are in good taste. Motels joined the taste craze by decorating their rooms and public areas in their own interpretation of the *House and Garden* color scheme of the season, however inappropriate that might be for their purpose. They appealed to the travelers to stay in rooms with "shaggy carpets, decorated in sun-drenched colors." Early-Pullman style gave way to twentieth-century motel, featuring Spanish furniture, wrought-iron table lamps, and hand-painted desert pictures. During the process, bath towels shrank 40 percent in size and a bar of soap became a wafer. Thus was American motel decor "Marriottized"; simple good taste became the victim of "richness" or gold-plated borax.

Ada Louise Huxtable, in *The New York Times*, expressed these sentiments eloquently when she wrote:

And yet I never approach a trip requiring an overnight stay without a sinking heart. It's not that I won't be reasonably comfortable—basic things like beds and baths and ice and Coke machines are the preoccupation of the American "Hospitality" industry—it's that I will be so depressed. It is that one is forced into a banal, standardized, multi-billion-dollar world of bad colors, bad fabrics, bad prints, bad pictures, bad furniture, bad lamps, bad ice-buckets, and bad wastebaskets of such totally uniform and cheap consistency of taste and manufacture that borax or camp would be an exhilarating change of pace.

A century ago, craftsmen and small retailers were in close touch with their customers, but with the loss of eye-to-eye relationships, manufacturers have been forced to conduct research programs to determine the changing directions of customers' tastes. The industrial system cannot afford a trial-and-error marketing program, so it must reduce its risks on new products by extensive and expensive test-marketing. Once a clue to the trends is discerned from the tests, then the manufacturers employ all of the techniques of advertising and sales promotion to influence public taste and to create a demand for things which, on occasion, the public never knew it wanted.

Television has proved to be the most persuasive of all selling tools, often with unfortunate results to public taste. The attire of television stars frequently has misled the viewers by encouraging them to believe that the revealing gowns of Cher and the bizarre outfits of Doc Severinsen were "in," as they failed to recognize the theatrical requirement of overstatement for dramatic effects.

Who are the tastemakers? The Beautiful People reported in *Women's Wear Daily*? The fashion magazines? Designers? Stores? Any of them can be; all of them are not. The BP, as wealthy socialites, exercise a taste influence, except when their hedonism transgresses the bounds of good taste. Fashion magazines forfeit their position as taste leaders when they become obsessed with the necessity to be first to report the new, whether it is good or bad, and when they sell out their editorial pages to their advertisers. They become reporters of the products of their advertisers rather than critics of fashion and taste.

The fashion business, unlike the theater or architecture, has no professional critics (like Walter Kerr or Ada Louise Huxtable) to review the fashion collections and express editorial opinions. Instead, it has hundreds of reporters, many without adequate fashion backgrounds, who cover all of the openings and relay the news on hemlines, fullness of skirts, and the newest eye makeup. *Women's Wear Daily* was the only publication that attempted a critic's role in recent years, but it made the mistake of mixing its criticisms and its editorial point of view with the news stories. *WWD* now sticks to reporting, which it does with thoroughness and skill.

Designers, with their sensitivity to the undercurrent of ideas, bring artistic understanding and fresh solutions that affect taste in clothes, furniture, decor, and automobiles. They could benefit from honest and fair criticism, though they probably would resent it just as the theater does. The reason why it has not been tried is probably related to the large amount of advertising dollars the fashion industry spends in the papers and magazines and its regard for publicity stories of new products and fashion-show reviews or advance stories as their just due. No publisher wants to kill Santa Claus.

When the history of taste of the twentieth century is written, I anticipate that the department and specialty stores of Europe and the United States will be credited with having made the single largest contribution to the formation and, at times, the improvement of mass taste. The public has more frequent experiences with stores than with any other types of business or cultural institutions. Admission is free and, with the exception of a few of the old-time formidable saleswomen, there is nothing inhibiting or forbidding about wandering from floor to floor to see the wonders of the world—brass from the Turkish bazaars, foods from the Middle East, porcelains from the Orient, fashions from the best designers of both continents. It's the greatest free show on earth.

The shopper or looker might witness a fashion show and be able to observe the manner in which the clothes have been accessorized and how the designers have used fresh color combinations, or see a new group of model rooms inspired by Brazil or a collection of Vasarely paintings. Forty years ago, I borrowed twenty canvasses by Gauguin from private collectors and commissioned a series of ball gowns by leading designers in the colors of the painter's Tahitian series. It proved to be a tremendous success, with a sellout of the clothes and the arousal of a vast amount of public interest. The large part of the Dallas public had never before seen an original Gauguin, much less twenty. Art lovers from all over the state came especially to see the pictures; school-teachers brought their entire classes to view the exhibition. Most important of all was the fact that thousands who didn't know anything about Gauguin were exposed to his paintings unwittingly and went away enriched, at no cost. Twenty years later, a curator at the Museum of Modern Art in New York came up to me and told me that the birth of her interest in art came from a visit to the Gauguin show at Neiman-Marcus which her teacher had taken her class to see.

With the liberal use of art in our stores and with our successful fashion promotions built around art themes, many people have wondered why we never added an art gallery to our group of luxury departments. "You and your brothers have such a keen interest in art, it seems that a gallery would be a natural," they would say. Perhaps that is one of the reasons we didn't—because, with differing tastes in art among the brothers, that would have been a sure way to precipitate a family quarrel.

I guess the real reason, though, has been the fact that as retailers we have been used to dealing in absolutes: the largest stocks of the choicest furs, the finest assortment of diamonds, the most comprehensive collections of couture clothes. In art, such a policy is impossible; a dealer has to decide in which field he will specialize. So we decided against becoming art dealers and to content ourselves with being modest collectors instead.

To be a tastemaker, you have to have good taste, but having good taste does not necessarily make you a tastemaker. In addition to good taste, the tastemaker must have the self-confidence and some of the arrogance of Cézanne. All of which leads up to three gentlemen—Hoving, Zabar, and Gucci—who have a lot in common. The three of them are merchants in noncompetitive fields; two of them have large operations, and one has a tiny business. All three are perfectionists, idealists, money-makers, and they are arrogant in their conviction that they know what is best for their customers. They are tastemakers.

Walter Hoving, former chairman of Tiffany & Co., is a veteran retailer whose previous retail experience at Montgomery

Ward, Macy's, Lord & Taylor, and Bonwit Teller gave him an earned right to have very definite opinions about the retail business, its merchandise, and its customers. Not only did he express his convictions with a certain degree of arrogance but he practiced them at Tiffany's with success.

Although he never proclaimed himself a tastemaker, I suspect that he would accept the title without undue immodesty. He established the Tiffany Design Award, which is "based on the principle that a comprehensive and distinguished design program cannot merely be left to designers, no matter how good they are. The chief executive himself must want it, must initiate it, and must enthusiastically support it throughout its development." He took a backhand slap at competition by commenting, "The basis of good design is sincerity. The enemy of good design is pretense."

In an interview in *Women's Wear Daily*, Hoving outdid the famous Charles Wilson statement that "what's good for the country is good for General Motors, and vice versa" by saying, "Give the customer what Tiffany likes, because what it likes, the public ought to like."

He took a dim view of the current merchandising efforts of the Fifth Avenue stores which are willing to stock anything that will sell; he contends that only Gerry Stutz at Bendel's has a consistent point of view in the operation of her store. While president of Lord & Taylor, he made daily trips to the various departments and reviewed a rack of $49.95 dresses one day, a counter of $25.00 handbags the next. As a result of this close personal interest in the contents of a stock, the buyers got to know what management wanted. "When I was at L & T," he said, "we established the concept that our look was to be classic and well-bred. We didn't permit the buyers to deviate from that objective." *WWD* quoted him: "Sometimes you mustn't pay too much attention to your customers. That's the best way to mess up your merchandise."

In answer to the customer who wanted men's diamond rings, which Tiffany refused to sell, he said, "What you want is your business. What we sell is our business." Not even Marie Antoinette had that much arrogance. She merely said, "Let them eat cake"; Hoving told them to stuff it.

Taste

Eli Zabar is a thirty-five-year-old food merchant who deals in the finest products that he can find or make himself; quite appropriately his establishment is named E.A.T. His small shop is located at 1064 Madison Avenue, New York, with a twiglet operation at Henri Bendel. He is the youngest son of the Zabar family of New York delicatessen fame, and decided several years ago that Zabar's was too big and successful to accommodate his ego and innovative ideas about food. He is a zealot for quality, driving fifty miles to Connecticut to pick up four cartons of a superior watercress or going to a remote village above Grasse, France, to persuade an olive grower to sell him his oil.

He underwent no professional food training, so he had nothing to unlearn; he is self-taught and, considering his gastronomic accomplishments, he must be a very quick learner. Self-confidence he has, in superabundance, as indicated by his statement: "I am completely confident of what I can do, for I am in perfect harmony as an artist, a creator, and a businessman." Whenever he tastes a great dish in a restaurant, he takes it as a personal challenge to improve it. He claims: "My greatest success is the last thing I did and the next thing I will do."

He has trained the palates of his customers to his own sense of taste; he creates new taste sensations by his constant experimentation; he has given his customers a standard of the best taste in all the products he sells, making it difficult for them ever again to be satisfied with second best.

Hoving's arrogance might have been born out of the self-confidence of experience; Zabar's brand of arrogance is the product of a virtuoso who has not yet taken his first course in humility. "I don't listen to anyone; I haven't the slightest interest in what any customer wants. If I satisfy myself, then there is no problem in pleasing them. No customer knows as much as I do. No one is as sensitive to the world I work in, or has the sensitivity and knowledge I have." His brashness would be unbearable if it were not for the fact that Eli Zabar is every bit as good as he proclaims himself to be.

Not everybody can take him, but he has attracted a clientele which appreciates his creativity, his devotion to quality, and his honesty. He admits, "I am so passionate and intense about what I do that I have a fight almost every day." Once when I was in his shop, I witnessed his fight of the day; and though my whole training has been to placate customers, I had to admire his spunk if not his wisdom.

A well-dressed man came in while I was talking to Eli and requested a bottle of olive oil. He was shown the oil from France made by the Moulin de la Braque, which Zabar imports exclusively to the United States. When the customer was told it was $10, he exclaimed loudly that no oil was worth that price. Zabar opened the bottle and gave him a spoon to taste it. "Well, that tastes like Mazola," he declared, "but, I'll take it anyway, even though you are overcharging me." "No you won't," said Zabar. "I won't sell it to you, and I would appreciate it if you never come back here again."

Zabar loves what he is doing and so do his customers. When his store opened five and one-half years ago, there were no others like it in the country. He has been paid the dubious honor, now, of having been copied. Today, there are twenty similar stores in New York City alone. They can copy the stores, but an arrogant genius like Eli Zabar comes along only at infrequent intervals.

To the best of my knowledge, the only retail store that ever rated a feature story in *New York* magazine was Gucci. The piece was titled, "The Rudest Store in New York," in which Mimi Sheraton recited chapter and verse of the common complaints about New York's busiest retail operation. From 1965, when Gucci opened on Fifth Avenue, until the time of this article in November 1975, Gucci had scored the most successful quality-merchandising achievement of the postwar period, and had proved that rudeness and arrogance to customers paid off.

Gucci rudeness was a common topic of conversation among shoppers, so the *New York* story was not news to anyone, with the possible exception of its president, Dr. Aldo Gucci, who, "a Milanese friend told me, was called, in certain circles *L'Imperatore*," according to Ms. Sheraton. Great a merchant as he is, and I consider him one of the best of this generation, it is hard to believe that he was unaware of his staff's attitude or that he had not encouraged it. He may have believed in the philosophy, quoted by Ms. Sheraton, that "at Gucci they seem to think that if Americans are treated like dirt, they will buy more."

Ms. Sheraton wrote:

Just as four generations of this Florentine family have perfected techniques of leathercraft, so the sales staff has mastered with equal impeccability the art of the drop-dead put-down and the icy stare.

She concludes her indictment with this final paragraph:

Gucci rudeness, then, would seem to be a combination of factors, not forgetting the possibility of overworked, underpaid help resenting customers who can afford to buy the merchandise. The main cause, however, is undoubtedly a reflection of what Dr. Gucci considers to be pride, but which the rest of the world recognizes as arrogance.

Following the appearance of this devastating critique there was a noticeable improvement in the attitude of the salespeople, but it would be a bit of hyperbole to describe Gucci service by the word "gracious." As is its privilege, the company has clung to some of its criticized operating policies, such as noonday closings and tight restrictions on the return of merchandise for credit.

Dr. Gucci, a voluble, trim-looking man of seventy-two, looks like a Florentine, dresses like a Milanese, and uses his hands like a Neapolitan, with his gestures preceding his words. He modestly describes himself as having the ambitions of a poet and not of a businessman, but his record tends to prove that his business acumen in selecting real estate and markets for expansion is about as perfect as it could be. As a poet, he has given his business a lyrical standard of good taste and fine quality that is unsurpassed in Europe and the United States. Of all of his ventures, Paris is the only one that could be characterized as less than a smashing success. He brushes aside this slight defeat in a deprecating way by commenting, "The French are funny people."

He has had the courage to build beautiful, luxurious stores and stock them lavishly with fine-quality merchandise that consistently follows his taste. While other stores are diluting the value of their own names by the promotion of designers' names, Gucci is the only label to be found in his stores. Not only that, but a good portion of the articles displayed have some variation of the *G* for Gucci embodied in their design. His intimate knowledge of the manufacturing process has enabled him to maintain the quality of his goods despite a general market deterioration.

At a time when many retailers are trying to popularize their institutions by lowering price lines, Dr. Gucci is instituting a new private gold-key club where his most affluent customers can select their expensive gifts away from the throngs which jam the Gucci selling floors during gift-giving periods. Gucci handbags and shoes have become status symbols to the public, which has been so impressed with the Gucci look that it has been willing to overlook less than ideal sales assistance.

I once asked Dr. Gucci if he could detect any difference in merchandise acceptance between his European and American stores. He replied, "When a woman is elegant and has taste she needs no passport."

Taste, good *or* bad, always exists, but it is never static or permanent. Taste which may be good to one generation is very likely to seem bad to the next, and then may return to favor twenty-five years later. This is demonstrated in clothes, decoration, architecture, and art. Paintings which were virtually hooted off the walls in France in the nineteenth century now fetch a million dollars or more at auction. Perhaps their prices will sag in the twenty-first. Collectors were not ready for the new concept of vision of the Impressionist painters; their minds could not appreciate what they saw. As a consequence of this misjudgment, subsequent generations of collectors vowed they would not similarly be caught off guard and have embraced many a meretricious art movement, hoping to get in on the ground floor and to demonstrate the perspicacity of their taste.

Fashion and taste are interrelated, for as fashion changes, new taste appraisals must be made. Fashion moves at a fast pace; changes in taste are slower because the eye must become accustomed to new forms, color combinations, innovative methods of expression. Fashion, in clothes particularly, is a reflection of the psychological and economic needs of society at any given time. Taste is the filtering device that screens out the fads and eccentricities, and eventually gives authority and legitimacy to the fashion. Here are two examples: "hot pants" came onto the fashion horizon in the late sixties, but good taste ruled them out as a fashion, so they became a fad, having both a meteoric rise and descent; blue jeans started off as workclothes and were first adopted by the young for daily wear, later by all ages as taste gradually gave them approval. They have become America's greatest fashion contribution to people all over the world.

The relationship of fashion and taste is explained well by James Laver, who wrote: "Fashion is not an inanimate object, and it is never at rest, a distinction it shares with life itself, of which it seems to be some special and significant manifestation. Fashion, in short, is a spearhead of taste, or rather it is a kind of psychic weathercock which shows which way the wind blows, or even a weathercock with the gift of prophecy, which shows which way the wind will blow tomorrow."

John Corry, in a whimsical and thoughtful column in *The New York Times*, "That Elusive Thing Called Taste," wrote:

Good taste is frequently handed down by fiat, or to be more accurate, through osmosis. This, however, can be tricky because what is being handed down may not necessarily be good taste; it may only be fashion. Sometimes the fashion is in good taste; sometimes it is not. Sometimes the fashion is in neither good nor bad taste, but exists only in a neutral ground. What can you say about Farrah Fawcett-Majors' hair, Arnold Schwarzenegger's muscles, or Andy Warhol's tomato cans? You can only say that they are there.

Blunders in taste are as obvious to the initiated as errors in grammar are to the educated. How, then, does one become taste-conscious; what are the methods of taste-cultivation? There are some who have good taste in specialized fields, such as typography, art, or flower arrangement, and show no evidence of taste in their clothes or their homes. In such cases, I suspect that the individuals just haven't paid any attention to areas other than their specialized fields.

I knew a dress designer who made beautiful clothes, but neglected her personal appearance. It was hard to imagine that this frowsy, unkempt woman with runners in her drooping stockings was capable of the creation of beauty. Bill Blass, on the other hand, is the epitome of good taste in both the clothes he wears and those he designs.

A person can seek taste development in one field, such as fashion or decoration, or in all fields simultaneously, since the basic principles of taste apply to all. I would recommend general exposure. The beginner should read such publications as *Women's Wear Daily*, or its sister, *W*, and the fashion and home magazines, which all report the latest developments in fashion, even though they make little evaluation of the taste factors. Visits to stores, private homes opened for charity, museums, and going to fashion shows are all useful in training the eye to see as well as to look, and in helping to cultivate a sense of discrimination. Retrospective shows demonstrate how painters established varied color relationships at different points of their careers, and how their tastes evolved.

WWD and *W* publish annually an illustrated list of IN and OUT fashions which, if carefully studied, offer some clues toward changes in taste as well as in fashion. Prominent people of stage and society are often photographed and this might lead cynics to wonder if the subjects shown in OUT fashions were picked for a *WWD* vendetta purpose. The yearly Best Dressed list may offer some good prototypes to emulate, but social politics, rather than merit, are often the basis for election to this list.

The eye responds to the process of constant looking, of comparing one article or period of design with another, of reviewing numerous exhibitions in rapid order. Reading about the things that have been seen reinforces what has been learned by observation. I've noticed that young people with no visible indications of taste quickly begin to develop taste from the objects they handle, the fashion shows they see, and the examples set by their associates. Once the eye has been trained, periodic exercise is necessary to maintain critical sharpness.

Simplicity is the keynote of much of the greatest art in the world, and simplicity is the basic starting point for anyone getting into taste education. Even a sequined dress can be simple. Simplicity in clothes or architecture serves as a foil for a baroque ornamentation; oversimplicity results in blandness, overdecoration in chaos. The study of books designed by Bruce Rogers and Daniel Updike, the clothes by Chanel and Balenciaga, the architecture of Louis Sullivan and Mies van der Rohe will impart the great lessons of simplicity and fitness; a search for their current counterparts will be rewarding.

For a person lacking in taste-confidence in clothes, the best solution is to locate a salesperson in a good shop who can be depended on to give honest and candid advice. If the customer frankly states the problem, the price limitations, and desires, such a salesperson will work doubly hard to fulfill the trust. The bluffers or the phonies are detected very quickly by any experienced salesperson, who is then likely to give them the "quick freeze."

Wealth does not always carry taste with it, for on the way up the financial and social ladder, many people had neither the time nor the interest to cultivate their taste. The most conspicuous example of this is the clothes worn by many wives of the well-dressed chief executives of the largest corporations in the nation. Nowhere have I observed less tastefully dressed women than at large banquets given by their husbands. Some large companies recognize this problem, and on occasion have commissioned Neiman-Marcus to counsel the wives of rising young executives and assist them in meeting the taste challenges of new social environments brought about by their husbands' promotions in the corporate hierarchy.

The taste of individuals in different fields of expression is not always the same. For example, Philip Johnson, the famous architect, is a man of meticulous taste in everything he does; in his personal attire he is ultraconservative and in his architectural taste and art collecting he is avant-garde. When I commented on this to him, he shyly replied, "What about you?" He had me, for despite my dedication to contemporary art and architecture, I, too, am a conservative in dress. I don't like wearing a patterned tie on a patterned shirt. I find that a solid-color tie is noncompetitive and seems to anchor the design of the shirt. I would never recommend that a person wear anything which feels strange; it's not good taste to be uncomfortable.

What then is the chemistry of this mysterious and abstract quality called taste? Who are the chemists? Where are their credentials? These would have been easy questions to answer a few centuries ago when there was an aristocratic society whose leaders bestowed the sanctions, but it is more complex in today's democratic world. In the days of royalty, it was the queen or a powerful mistress and members of the court; in the twentieth century, it is a mysterious "they" who set the taste standards in the Western world. It would be difficult to put names on the "they" group, for they are not appointed by any authority, nor elected to position, nor concentrated in any one particular country, nor do they have meetings, nor do they conduct polls. Moreover, the composition of their membership may change from one decade to another.

Their ultimate approbation or rejection of a shift in taste is final and without appeal—at least until different social and political conditions warrant reconsideration. There are different "theys" for fashion, decor, architecture, automobiles, manners, table-settings, and dozens of other subjects. Some have a multinational influence, others function nationally, and, as an example, the "theys" in Japan consider it good taste for a diner to use a toothpick at the table if he shields his mouth and hand behind a napkin. The "theys" in the United States and Europe think it bad taste to use a toothpick at the table, with or without benefit of a napkin, despite the opinion of dental hygienists to the contrary.

In the South, "they" approve the eating of fried chicken with the hands; in sections of the country where fried chicken is not a regional dish, hands are tabooed in favor of fork and knife. Internationally, "they" use white, gray, and light blue stationery; "they" do not consider red, dark brown, and purple correct. "They" give acceptance to the fashion of a low décolleté but not to the transparent, see-through gowns. "They" serve dinner on bone china and luncheon on earthenware, not vice versa.

"They" are men and women whose taste is favorably recognized by the public as being trustworthy; some are nonprofessionals, others are designers, fashion editors, socialites. There is a variety of different age "they" groups, but the most influential at the present are the young, under-twenty "theys" and those in the twenty-five–to–forty bracket. The young "theys" overwhelmingly endorsed the taste of the blue-jean fashion as being good taste for themselves, despite the disagreement of the older "theys," who eventually capitulated.

Public opinion is generally regarded as representing a nontabulated majority; "they" certainly cannot be defined as a majority, but rather as a forceful, influential minority, whose opinion carries great authority. What this group does, its peers will accept, and most others will gradually emulate. Only a few iconoclasts want to buck "they."

Sir Kenneth Clark, the art historian and critic, makes a pertinent observation on taste in his memoir, *The Other Half:*

It has become fashionable to say that the words "good taste" are meaningless. The people who say this, often quite clever people, should be compelled to buy all their carpets and curtains in a co-operative store.

There are some who exaggerate the importance of taste, who make it a shrine at which they worship. That, of course, is pure nonsense. A person with bad or indifferent taste can live a perfectly happy and normal life, have a loving family, and be financially successful. Good taste, like education, simply opens new opportunities for the enjoyment of life.
I know about this firsthand, for I spent my business life

in the operation of a business dedicated to the distribution of quality merchandise in good taste. I found it both profitable and pleasurable to supervise the quality and taste of the merchandise we sold and, thereby, to earn the loyalty of customers who appreciated our standards. They bought from us because they got their money's worth, because the surroundings pleased them, because they liked our taste. They phoned us to find out the correct length of gloves to wear for a particular social occasion; they came to us for counsel on what to wear with what. Our objective was to send them out properly attired, correctly accessorized—always in good taste, so that they could wear their clothes with assurance.

Brides and mothers-of-the-bride, particularly, are beset with problems, but rarely does the father-of-the-bride ask for help. One day, though, I received a phone call from a father-of-the-bride who was so overwhelmed by the magnitude of the occasion that he wanted us to design five dinner jackets for him to wear to five successive prenuptial parties. I advised him that even though we would like to make the sale, there weren't that many designs for tuxedos in good taste and that he should wear the same jacket to all of the parties. "Besides which," I said, "you're not the star of the occasion—your daughter is." I told him I'd send him five different boutonnieres with my compliments instead. This satisfied him, and he has never stopped telling the story of how I turned down a five-suit sale. I earned his respect when he recognized that I placed good taste ahead of a profit.

As the head of Neiman-Marcus, I directed the efforts of a merchandising and buying staff in the procurement of the finest-quality merchandise in the world, as well as serving as its final taste arbiter. I covered the international markets myself in search of the best, the rare, the esoteric—in part because I relished the excitement of the hunt, and in part to maintain the kind of familiarity with world production that enabled me to give our buyers proper guidance and moral support. We always found a market for the best.

André Simon, the late wine authority and writer, put it aptly when he wrote in his book *Food*, "Taste is a matter of choice; but quality is a matter of fact."

Habit de Foureur,

A Paris, Chez N. de L'Armessin, Rüe S.t Jacques, à la Pôme d'Or, Avec Privil. du

5

Search for the Best:
The Things You Love to Touch

Whereas good taste need not necessarily be expensive, top quality costs more than other grades. In some cases, supply of the best is restricted by natural scarcity; in others, high costs limit demand to the point that there is no pressure to increase supply. If there were sufficient demand, theoretically, there would be twelve Claridges, fifty Maxim's, and a million Rolls-Royces. Most goods and services are automatically regulated by the factors of supply and demand, although the supply and the prices of diamonds are carefully controlled by the diamond syndicate. Auctions, supposedly, are the best indicators of free market prices, but there have been too many cases of collusive bidding on stones to accept auction prices as being conclusive.

Rarely have I found an article of superb quality in the hands of an unknowledgeable seller, for travel and communication has educated almost everyone everywhere. In the Jordanian section of Jerusalem, before the six-day war, I was bargaining for some archaeological objects with an unpretentious merchant in a run-down little shop. I suggested a price. The dealer said, "Wait a minute." He went behind a curtain in the rear of the premises and emerged a few minutes later with a Sotheby catalogue and, turning to a marked page, remarked, "See, pieces like this sold at Sotheby's last month for twice the price you are offering." The days of finding a bargain anywhere in the world are over, for most people have been made aware of current market values by the press, travelers, and the auctions. Every year, though, a story appears in the London *Times,* with almost suspicious regularity, about an astute buyer's discovery and purchase of a small Raphael painting or a drawing by da Vinci in an antique shop or in the attic of a country manor for a fraction of its real worth. One may wonder cynically if these finds are baits put out by the London Antique Dealers Society to fan the fires of hope in collectors' breasts.

Many wealthy customers would like to believe that whatever they may be buying is the finest of its kind in the world, and, of course, there are always salesmen who are only too willing to give them that assurance to make the sale. Early in my career as a fur buyer, I was ordering a fur coat from Joe De Leo, a dealer, who had the reputation for being both the best designer and the most expensive manufacturer in the business. After telling him I had a customer who wanted the finest mink coat in the world, he brought from his vaults his twenty top bundles. I examined them carefully, but knowing the nature of fur dealers, I said, "Joe, don't you have anything finer? A bundle, maybe, that you're saving for your wife?" "Well," he replied, "I do have a bundle I was going to make up for Mrs. De Leo, but how did you know?" I knew, because this is an old dodge to get the buyer to pay an extra price to the furrier to compensate for the sentimental wrench in parting with the skins.

After satisfying myself that this bundle was the finest, I asked, addressing him formally to dignify and give importance to the nature of my request, "Mr. De Leo, would it be possible to make this coat finer?" expecting to be reassured that the skins would make a garment representing the zenith of his career, the *ne plus ultra* of the furrier's skill, the ultimate in achievement. He nodded his head appreciatively. "Yes, it's always possible to make something better." "But we are already paying you an arm and a leg for your best bundle," I complained. "What more would it take to make it better?"

The usually fiery Joe De Leo was patient as he explained, "This coat will take sixty-two skins if I make it the normal deluxe way, eliminating the necks, much of the flanks, and the upperpart of the paws. If I should cut out even more of the sides and the rump, I would have to add possibly another ten skins, and there's no end to what you can keep on cutting away. Not only is there added skin cost but extra labor as well. I am already using a pure-silk lining, costing ten dollars a yard, but I guess there's no limit to what you can pay for a lining. The trouble is that it might cost more but not be as appropriate. So much for the manufacturing part. This bundle was matched out of a lot of twenty-five hundred skins, and we all think the grader did a fine job. There won't be any more skins this year, but if your customer is willing to wait until next year, we may be able to improve the grading a little bit; at the end of five years we could probably improve both color and texture twenty-five percent, but by that time your customer may be dead, and you've lost your sale.

"This coat will be fine enough for anybody alive, but just remember there is always a way to make anything finer, given time, money, and understanding." This was an important lesson for me to learn, and one that I have put to good use. Whenever I am asked, "Is this the best?" I am careful to reply, "This is the best available at this time," or "This is the best within commercial possibilities." So, as we discuss the search for the best, or the finest, let those terms be understood within the limitations set forth by Joe De Leo.

Even though I told the story of shahtoosh in my previous book, *Minding the Store*, I am repeating it because this fabric is indisputably the finest cloth of its kind in the world. During the war I kept hearing stories from pilots returning from India of a gossamer fabric made from the feathers of the Siberian goose. When I made my first trip to India, I searched for this feather textile without success, but then a helpful merchant suggested I take a look at a piece of shahtoosh, which he described as being so fine that a fifty-four-inch-wide shawl could be pulled through a wedding ring. Hence its name, "the ring shawl."

Finally, I found some shahtoosh and was astonished at the

Search for the Best: The Things You Love to Touch

77

fineness of the fiber, which makes it possible to weave it into the thinnest and warmest of all fabrics. Made in five- to seven-yard shawls, it serves wealthy Indian women as winter wraps; in fact, shahtoosh is the Indian woman's mink coat. I had it cut into proper size for men's mufflers, and I cherish the one I wear as probably my most luxurious possession. "Shah" means ruler and "toosh" means cloth, so the name shahtoosh translates into "cloth of the king." The fiber comes from the neck hair of the ibex goats which inhabit the upper slopes of the Himalayas. The animals descend to the timberline in the spring to forage on the tender leaves of the low-growing trees. In the process, they leave a lot of their neck hairs on the branches. The native women gather the hairs and spin them into yarn, from which the sheer cloth is handwoven. It is so fine that it makes other luxury cloths like vicuña and cashmere seem almost coarse by comparison. The supply is limited, and the demand, which I was partially responsible for creating, has forced the price up to about $1500 a yard in the United States, making it the most expensive fabric in the world as well as the finest. Few, if any, merchants have the courage to stock it, so you will have difficulty finding it.

If, however, you were to desire other precious-fiber fabrics, you would go to the little village of Borgosesia, northwest of Milan, where there's a textile mill dedicated to making the finest woolen fabrics in the world. The name of the mill is Agnona, and its founder and presiding genius is a small, ebullient man, Francesco Ilorini Mo. His order book reads like a "Who's Who in Fashion," for he has been a supplier to all of the top designers in the field of fashion. Balenciaga was the first to appreciate his quality; now he sells to Saint Laurent, Dior, Valentino, Mila Schön, Galanos, Trigère, Blass, Oxxford Clothes, and Jack Lenor Larsen for decorative textiles.

Ilorini is a sixteenth-century artisan-weaver working with twentieth-century machines that he has completely mastered. As a textile designer, he has an intimate knowledge of the capabilities and limitations of his looms; as a technician, he has a personal acquaintance with the characteristics of the fibers coming from animals all over the world. He started his own factory to make the finest and has never compromised with this objective during his career. He has made all the money he wants, but works with undiminished fervor out of regard for the three hundred people in his mill who have devoted their lives to the production of the finest in cloth.

In 1968, he made his first trip to Peru to get a firsthand knowledge of the native animals which produced the so-called precious fibers and he fell in love with the vicuñas, llamas, and alpacas he saw on the ranges, even to bringing back a baby llama for a pet, as well as bales of fleeces. He is so enamored with nature's own colors of white, beige, tan, and gray that he is reluctant to dye them, preferring to use them "as is" or in mixture with one another. In the actual weaving of the yarns of the South American fibers, he tries to retain the look of how they grow on the animal's back.

His vicuña fabric was the most beautiful and costly produced, until the animal was declared an endangered species and international restrictions forbade the manufacture or sale of cloth made from its fleece. The final two precious fibers come from China—cashmere and camel's hair, which are woven with greater skill and perfection on his looms than by any of the historic mills in Scotland.

But he weaves many other cloths as well, such as sheer wool voiles, silk-and-wool dress fabrics, tuxedo suitings, drapery materials, scarves, and shawls. He has never used synthetic fibers, nor blends of them with wool, and I am confident he never will, for he has a unique clientele to whom price is a secondary consideration. He has too great a respect for nature's products to tamper with them. Whereas most weavers wash their cloths thoroughly to remove the lanolin from the wool, he tries to retain as much natural oil as possible. He remarks, "Nature never betrays you—it always comes back"—in reference to the springy quality of wool which helps a garment maintain its shape.

Ilorini is a unique character in the machine age. He started as a textile worker when he was eleven years old and worked his way up through every phase of the industry. He met the machine and mastered it. I asked him his secret. His reply was forthright, as he is: "Keep in contact with the best, seek out other people who are engaged in the best, and search for the best." But, above all, he does it with devotion to an ideal.

He means it when he says, "We make our cloth with such love, we hate to see it go."

Cashmere first came into use in the fifteenth century in Kashmir, India, whence this softness of goat fleece got its name. It was used there in the making of shawls. Then, in the nineteenth century, the Empress Eugénie, wife of Napoleon III, who was a great fashion innovator, introduced the cashmere shawl to the French court, where it became an instantaneous success. Cashmere appeals to the tactile sense; men and women both enjoy stroking a cashmere sweater and luxuriating in its feel on their bodies. The cashmere fiber is so thin that it takes about two miles of this very fine yarn, or the fleeces of three goats, to make one average-size man's pullover. Increasing consumer affluence has created an ever-growing demand, which the Chinese have recognized by charging more and more for the "golden fleece." A fine cashmere sweater in 1978 will sell for upward of $100, or ten times the price of 1938.

Cashmere sweaters have long been regarded as one of the world's most luxurious articles of wearing apparel, and since their introduction in 1920, they have always commanded a price in excess of other sweaters on the market. First made by the Scottish underwear mills in Hawick as boxy, unadorned pullovers and cardigans, they were soon knitted on full-fashion machines to ensure better fit. Competition became so intense on classic sweaters that the mills hired name designers to create different textures, collars, necklines, and shapes. In the late twenties, the Ballantyne Mills introduced intarsia designs requiring the use of a hand machine to inlay the front of the sweater with geometric and floral patterns.

Increased world demand for all natural fibers has had the effect of reducing quality. Competition from mills in Japan and South America has broken the monopoly once held by Britain in worsted fabrics. Higher prices for yarns and increased interest rates in financing them have forced weavers to search for faster machines, putting the yarns under much greater tension. One of the few fabrics that is finer today than ever before is that called "100's," made from the belly fleece of the Australian Geelong merino sheep, which have been bred to produce fleeces of superior quality to that produced by standard breeds. So fine is it that one hundred fibers occupy the space of one inch. One pound of spun thread would be fifty-six thousand yards long. Hence the name "100's." When woven, the yarn makes the finest quality of worsted fabrics. The supply is limited; it is more expensive to manufacture, and the price is approximately 30 percent higher than other fine-quality worsteds. It is the true aristocrat of men's suitings, available at a limited number of stores and custom tailors. Lumb's in England are reputed to be the most reliable spinners of this quality yarn.

Solid-color fabrics are the most difficult to produce without flaws, and the finer the yarn, the more difficult it is to attain perfection. In most cases, slubs in a worsted cloth may be caused by the breaking of the thread on the loom and the subsequent knotting of the ends. In the case of yarn-dyed fabrics, as compared to those dyed after being woven, a subtle gradation of tone between different skeins of yarn can cause a slight but noticeable shading in the fabric. At some point in textile history, some smart weaver had the brilliant and original idea to put a stripe in a solid-color fabric, thus making any imperfection less perceptible. Patterned cloths were born as a result of this successful experiment, and the same reasoning was applied to both silk and cotton—designs were printed on them to obscure either a shoddy or imperfect material. Interestingly, prints became so important in fashion that the original reason for making them does not necessarily apply today.

Earlier, I referred to the great deterioration of quality in apparel, blaming both machine production and inflation. This is particularly true in the medium and high price ranges, with a few notable exceptions. Men's suits by Oxxford are made as fine today as when Louis Weinberg, the founder of the company, first set up the standards of Oxxford's quality. His successor, Jack McDonald, has been faithful to the originator's conceptions, and, if anything, he has improved on them. There isn't any men's clothing made in the world, by manufacturers or custom tailors, that challenges Oxxford's quality.

To give you an idea of what goes into the making of an

Oxxford suit, here is a list of some of the steps taken to attain that quality:

1. The garments are individually hand-cut with shears for precise accuracy and matching.
2. More and wider seams are provided.
3. The sack coat is given more preparatory or underpressings than any other make. The coat "hits the iron" thirty-two times while in the process of manufacture. The preparatory pressings are the cornerstone of Oxxford construction. Their purpose is to mold into the garment the shape acquired in sewing.
4. The Oxxford coat front—or hymo, or canvas, as it is sometimes called—the finest procurable, is thoroughly cold-water shrunk, hand-cut, hand-padded, and hand-sewn.
5. The collar and lapels are hand-padded with hundreds of fine stitches, to assure that the shape will be maintained for the life of the garment.
6. The armholes are drawn by hand with a chain backstitch for resiliency, which permits the armholes to give without stretching.
7. Double arm shields are provided, hand felled all the way around, not merely tacked.
8. The buttonholes are made by hand, and are worked on both sides of the opening.
9. The buttons, sewn on by hand with a strong shank, permit the garment to move freely even when buttoned.
10. The pockets have linen stays to prevent sagging, and a complete bellows lining on the inside to permit the pocket to expand to the inside rather than bulge to the outside.

The only area for improvement in the Oxxford product is in the construction and installation of jacket and trouser pockets that have a tendency to pull away from the suiting fabric in the corners and sometimes fringe along the seams.

In women's apparel, the clothes of James Galanos in the United States and Mila Schön in Milan represent garment-making at the height of perfection. Both they and Oxxford have been willing to accept the limitation of volume that their expensive merchandise imposes. All three had to make the choice between larger production with less hand labor at lower prices and a smaller business of top quality at higher prices. Almost every other maker made the decision to compromise, or was forced to do so by economic forces.

The great change in life-styles has had an effect on what women and men want in the clothes they wear. As Adele Simpson comments, "More and more, women are wearing less and less." Gone are figure-controlling girdles; gone are garter belts; half-gone are brassieres; going are petticoats and slips. The "sack" dress, born of Balenciaga, and the adoption of the Middle Eastern caftan were a reflection of women's desires for clothes that were less constrictive and more comfortable. The dress trade seized on these fashions greedily, for their simplicity of construction made them easier to produce, just as the menswear industry went all out for leisure suits requiring less skilled tailoring.

Lines like Galanos and Schön are not the ones you see most copied, for top-quality workmanship, unlike fashion, is impossible to imitate. You either make something as well as possible, and pay the price, or you don't. Saint Laurent and Dior clothes are reproducible at lesser prices—in look at least. Since these and other designer clothes are copied rapidly, due to weak or nonenforceable design-piracy laws, women are able to buy good, if not exact, versions of the originals within a short time after the clothes have made their debut.

The search for the best can lead to a lengthy and tortuous trail. Before World War II, I had purchased in France some handspun, handwoven, sheer-linen handkerchiefs for my personal use. On my first trip after the war, I attempted to locate similar qualities for resale, but without success. I was told that German officers had bought up all existing supplies and the workers had been so dispersed that it was unlikely that these luxury handkerchiefs would ever be made again. When I went to France on subsequent trips, I always made the same inquiry and invariably received the same answer. Finally, just a few years ago, I got a transatlantic call from our leading handkerchief supplier, who excitedly told me he had discovered a supply of prewar handkerchiefs of the type I had been requesting, which an old employee, now deceased,

*Search for
the Best:
The Things
You Love
to Touch*

had hidden away in a carton marked "Records 1934–5" to save them from the Germans. Because of my long-sustained interest, he offered me the entire lot of some five hundred men's and women's handkerchiefs.

The virtues of handspun, handwoven handkerchiefs lie completely in the sheerness and the feel to the hand and the nose. They are delicate and fragile and they are aesthetically gratifying. The women's handkerchief had to retail for about $12.50 and the larger size for men at $20.00; I was confident they would sell easily, but they didn't. Kleenex had just about killed the handkerchief business and the new, younger saleswomen, never having sold a handkerchief for anything like those prices, were hard to enthuse about them. Finally I got impatient with them and said: "You've had a year to sell these and you haven't really tried. I'm going to take them away from you and sell all of them myself."

I realized that the prospects for these handkerchiefs had to be wealthy customers and, in addition, had to have an appreciation for anything that was unusually fine. I compiled a list of men and women with these qualifications and wrote them this letter:

Dear Mrs. Carson:

This past spring when I was in France, I came across a group of prewar, handspun, handwoven handkerchiefs which one of our makers had just discovered stored away in an old records' carton. They are so rare that I bought the entire lot. Although the handkerchiefs are thirty to forty years old, linen does not deteriorate and they are in perfect color and condition, and are available as follows:

Men's handkerchiefs, 18" square	*$20.00 ea.*
Ladies' handkerchiefs, 10" square	*12.50 ea.*
Ladies' glove handkerchiefs, 7" square	*8.50 ea.*

If you would like to order any for Christmas gifts, I'd suggest that you write to us immediately, indicating the size and quantity desired.

Sincerely,
Stanley Marcus

The letter produced orders for over six hundred handkerchiefs, one hundred more than we had on hand. This success encouraged us to comb the markets for more, and, eventually, we found a cache of two hundred yards of fabric which the owner was keeping for his daughter's dowry. We persuaded him to swap the cloth for IBM stock as an equally suitable hedge against inflation.

Next in grade comes the machine-woven, 100 percent linen, made in France, Ireland, and Switzerland. It is heavier and sturdier, and wears much better than the delicate handspun variety. It is about one-fourth the price of the handwoven handkerchiefs. This is followed on the price scale by a handkerchief referred to in the trade as "chief value linen," a term used in the U.S. tariff book to designate a handkerchief, the chief value of which is a 53 percent linen content, thereby qualifying it for a lower duty rate than if it were made of all cotton. This blend makes a very satisfactory handkerchief at a moderate retail price. Finally, there is the Swiss 100 percent long-staple sheer cotton, called batiste, at the lowest price of any of the handkerchiefs made from natural yarns, despite its higher duty rate than those with chief value linen.

One of the earmarks of any fine handkerchief is a hand-rolled edge as compared to the less expensive and less attractive machine-stitched finish. Hand-rolling is the historical method of finishing both handkerchiefs and silk scarves, but, as hand labor has advanced in cost, both the availability and quality of hand-rolling has become a problem. Manufacturers in some countries have been forced to send articles as far away as the Philippines to get this work done.

Both high costs and changing tastes have all but eliminated the lace-trimmed and embroidered handkerchiefs of the eighteenth and nineteenth centuries. Today, the most fashionable handkerchiefs are unadorned, except for self-colored, corded borders and possibly a discreet hand-embroidered monogram. The stocks of the department stores are full of fancy machine-embroidered and machine-made lace-trimmed handkerchiefs at popular prices. In better stores, it is still possible to find an antique handkerchief with beautiful wide borders of handmade rose point or point d'esprit lace. These are museum pieces and are usually sold for a bridal trousseau or to lace collectors. They are one of the last vestiges of the Age of Elegance.

Along the quality trail, I found, strange as it may seem, that the growth in popularity of goat cheese had serious repercussions on the quality and availability of traditional fine kidskin gloves in France. That, together with increased cost of manufacturing and a general decline in the fashion importance of gloves, has cost France one of its traditional industries, one in which it surpassed the quality of production of all the other countries of Europe. The law of economic determinism has asserted itself: the demand for goat cheese has made it more profitable to raise more goats and kill fewer kids.

Modern technology has brought improvement in quality to numerous products, particularly those that come from laboratories. However, in the case of nature, new methods of feeding and chemical fertilization have had bad effects. Kids used to be fed by the mother goat's milk, which is now used for the production of cheese. The powdered milk being substituted causes bellyaches, damaging the belly portions of the skins.

Only a fraction of the previous glove production has stayed in France; most of it has fled to the Philippines, where kidskin gloves are now being made very well in factories operated by Germans.

The quality of gloves, like fur coats, is determined by the number of skins used, the amount of waste caused by skin defects, the fineness of the sewing, the skill and speed of the cutter. A glovecutter's production can vary from twelve pair a day to three or four dozen. The two sewing techniques most commonly used in France were the inseam method, whereby the several parts making the fingers were joined together by delicate, fine seams on the inside of the glove, and the French piqué method, in which a more rugged seam was made on the exterior. The former was favored for dress-wear and the latter for sports activities.

Women have always preferred kid and lambskin for dressy

occasions—often lined with fine silk jersey for warmth and greater luxury—and pigskin, wool or fur-lined, for driving and outdoor wear. Gloves have been made from reindeer, ostrich, chamois, horse, and even the dog. They have been decorated with lace, ribbons, gold bullion, monograms, and feathers. In the past, they have served for utility and decoration for both women and men. Today, fashion has frowned on the glove as an essential accessory in a woman's wardrobe and has relegated its use to driving and purposes of warmth. The U.S. male, unlike his European brother, never did wear gloves for any other reasons than warmth and protection.

The glove business has declined so sharply that many stores have eliminated the specialized job of the glove buyer and have assigned the responsibility as a tag-on job to some other buyer who has to go to Europe to buy scarves or handbags. The loss of the technically skilled professional glove buyer and her replacement by a scarf buyer, who also buys a few gloves, has further contributed to both the bad health of the industry and the poor glove selections in most stores. A customer seeking a fine pair of gloves might have to shop a number of stores before finding the type, the color, and the size desired.

The American shoe industry, which led the world for almost a century in the machine production of shoes, suddenly became the victim of foreign competition in the late sixties, when cheap labor in the Far East and more sophisticated manufacturing methods in Italy stole a substantial portion of the domestic market. Europe, and particularly Italy, always has had great shoe designers whose greatest strength has been their willingness to experiment. American makers were only too glad to copy their designs but, as David Evins says, "were stupid in their unwillingness to copy their technical methods." The quality shoe-manufacturing business in the United States disappeared in a period of five years. Virtually all fine shoes sold in the United States are produced in Italy and France, with a few being made in England. Secondary qualities are manufactured in Spain and Greece, and lesser grades in Brazil. The look of the European shoe is still great;

the quality has deteriorated. The Italians have yielded only grudgingly to the U.S. demand for varying widths, for their whole system of production has been predicated on single widths, as anyone who has ever bought a pair of shoes at Gucci can testify. As to sizes, the Italians apparently do not believe women wear size eleven.

The machine has supplanted the old-fashioned shoemaker, and the product, while looking superficially the same, is not the same and does not give a comparable degree of comfort as the handmade shoe. The custom shoemaker, who made shoes to measure, has all but disappeared. One of the few remaining is Lobb of London and Paris, who charges a minimum of $600 a pair to those who can afford them and are willing to wait months for delivery. An amusing story is told about an American who brought back a pair of Lobb shoes to be repaired when he visited Paris in 1925. He was given a claim check, but he didn't return to Paris until World War II. After the armistice, he remembered that he had the claim check in his wallet, so he dropped into Lobb's, introduced himself, and asked for his shoes. In a few minutes the salesman came back, and said, "Yes, we still have your shoes. If you will come back in three weeks, they will be ready."

Though the quality of leather has declined, makers of leather shoes and handbags agree that tanning and dyeing have improved enough to partially offset the loss in leather quality. When I asked M. Jean-Louis Dumas, *père,* one of the senior members of the great house of Hermès, "Are your bags as fine as they used to be?" he replied, "No, they are not; you're right. The workmanship is as fine as it ever was, but the quality of leather is not." When I asked the cause for this decline in leather, he discussed the impact of technological effects on the quality of many natural products, explaining that with the advent of chemically enriched feeding for cattle, the veins had become larger and more visible and the hides had less resiliency when stretched.

Hermès, one of the finest luxury shops in the world, was founded in 1837 by Thierry Hermès, a saddlemaker. Still owned and managed by descendants of the founder, it has grown and prospered because of a rigid adherence to original standards of quality, combined with a willingness to move with the times by replacing a declining demand for saddles and harnesses with broader merchandise selections. It employs about fifteen workers to produce approximately four hundred special orders for polo, hunting, and riding saddles. The business is owned by the three daughters of Emile-Maurice Hermès, grandson of the founder, and it is managed and directed by their husbands, children, and cousins. Hermès continues to manufacture a major portion of its leather products in-house; it prints its famous scarves and neckties in a factory which it controls in Lyons; it produces its own couture and *prêt-à-porter* collections and its perfumes. Watches, cutlery, and jewelry it buys from the finest producers of Switzerland and France. At Hermès the design is classic; the taste is conservative; the quality is impeccable— never is there the slightest compromise in quality. Each handbag is the product of a single artisan; every scarf is printed on unleaded Chinese silk, of an eighteen momme weight, in fourteen to twenty-five colors.

Theoretically, a nepotistic business like Hermès should have failed long ago, but it hasn't. It has survived and prospered because of, and not despite, the family. And, under the dynamic leadership of its young new managing director, Jean-Louis Dumas-Hermès, *fils*, it should reach even greater heights.

For the past forty years, up until the advent of the Carter administration, the most favored gifts for the president of the United States or the State Department to present to visiting chiefs of state have been objects of glass made by Steuben, many of which, time permitting, were specially commissioned and engraved. This has been high tribute to an American company, the quality of whose product is as fine or finer than any other in the world. The government was not alone in its patronage of Steuben, for corporate officials, looking for the finest American product to give important customers or to commemorate the retirement of a chairman of the board, have also turned to Steuben. Gift pieces can run anywhere from $2000 to $50,000, prices which President Carter is reported to consider excessive.

Although Steuben was founded in 1903, its modern history begins in 1933, when Arthur A. Houghton, Jr., nephew of the former U.S. ambassador to Germany and England and grandson of the founder of the Corning Glass Company, persuaded Corning's board of directors to let him set up Steuben as an independent subsidiary dedicated to the production of the finest glass in the world. The corporation was patient and absorbed the early years' losses, allowing Houghton and his equally young associates free rein. Undoubtedly, the fact that the Houghton family was the single largest stockholder had some influence on the decision. The success of Steuben has added to the prestige of the parent company, Corning Glass, which also must have benefited from technological advances made by Steuben. This accomplishment should serve as a worthy and inspiring example to other American industries too large to engage in production gambles; they could profit by having smaller, pilot operations that could provide both luster and experimentation.

Although there is considerable difference of opinion on the design merits of many of the Steuben objects, there is no dispute about the superior quality of glass achieved. While some of the foreign glassmakers have used the word "crystal" to describe the high lead content of their product, Steuben has stuck to the less pretentious word "glass."

Fine glassmaking begins with the objective of the factory owner and the skill of the workers. The trade is best learned under the apprentice system in which a senior gaffer teaches his younger helper by demonstration. Steuben is one of the few manufacturers in the United States which still uses apprentices. Union rules have placed impediments in the way of producing fine, handsome glass because of the constant efforts by the union to apply the rules of the pressed or machine-made glass divisions to the Steuben atelier. Sharp rises in the labor component of the costs have led Steuben to depart from its traditional method of production, in which one man made the entire object, to a system in which various aspects of production are sectionalized and different parts are made by specialists.

Engraving plays an important part in the design and decoration of Steuben glass, and, since this is a slow and tedious process, fewer and fewer young people enter the engraving trade. Only the apprentice system has enabled Steuben to overcome this bottleneck in production, a battle which is far from won. Glass, being transparent, shows any defects more obviously than any other product made. There is no such thing as a perfect piece of glass any more than there is a perfect fur coat; but there is constant supervision of the molten fluid to test for bubbles or seeds, resulting from imperfect mixing and melting, which could show up in the finished piece. If such defects do appear in the article, even after such precautions, it is broken and put back in the melting pot.

Glassmaking is one of the industries that has benefited from improved technology. The development of the "continuing" furnace has resulted in a more consistent mixture; platinum tubes and platinum wall linings of furnaces don't melt under the intense heat; laboratory testing of the molten mix has eliminated a lot of the guesswork from production.

An unadorned goblet must be absolutely free from any easily visible blemish, but if it is decorated with an overall gold design or if it is faceted, any minor defect will be obscured, just as the stripe pattern in a piece of cloth fools the eye. Baccarat, the famous French glassmaker, uses both methods, but it also makes the finest, thinnest "crystal" goblets in the world. This company has worldwide distribution, and enjoys some of the largest and most prestigious accounts in the business. The king of Morocco orders two thousand stems a year, and the shah of Iran once gave Baccarat a $7-million order for crystal chandeliers.

If I were buying stemware, I would choose Baccarat's "Perfection" goblet, paper-thin and fragile, above any other I know. If I were selecting a gift, I would look for a Steuben ashtray, or one of their pieces engraved with prisms, or any one of their graceful fruit or flower bowls. Both companies are the results of idealists. Baccarat is headed by the Comte René de Chambrun, a descendant of Lafayette, who has dedicated himself to preserve and enhance the reputation of his wife's family business.

Grand Ciseau

Cremot

bonnet à   Oreille

fouleur

Patte pour   Ciseau à Border

lisiere et   Aiguille
                            à tricoter

Habit de Bonnetier,

A Paris, Chez N. de L'Armessin, Rüe St Jacq. à la Pôme d'Or.   Avec Privil. du R.

6

Search for the Best: Bed and Board

When it comes to maintaining high standards of service, no industries have had a more difficult time than hotels and restaurants. During the years of the Depression, many hotel owners went bankrupt or were forced to permit their properties to become run-down. Most had to go through the wringer twice before the investments proved profitable. A standard maxim, "Only fools build hotels; wise men buy them at the foreclosures," became modified to, "Only fools build hotels or buy them at the bankruptcy sales; wise men buy them at the second or third foreclosure."

All of this changed with the advent of the war and a huge mobile population. Hotels became busy and profitable, encouraging entrepreneurs like Conrad Hilton, Ernest Henderson, Sr., and Charles Forte of England to start the Hilton, Sheraton, and the Forte hotels. These men and others brought uniformity of service, standardization of decor and menus to hotels across the country and around the world.

In the process of establishing efficient operations, they impersonalized their hotels and stamped out any semblance of visible management, even though the Hilton chain placed a copy of Hilton's book *Be My Guest* in the bedrooms and a hand-painted portrait of the founder in every lobby.

Postwar, the jet airplane revolutionized travel patterns,

making it possible for individuals to go to places they had only dreamed of visiting. This acceleration of tourist traffic demanded additional hotel facilities in every major city and in remote corners of the world. Improvements in highways led to the birth of "motels" requiring lesser capital investments, offering fewer services, and charging lower prices than hotels.

As soon as the new hotels were built there came the realization that they had to be kept well-occupied, and one of the surest ways to accomplish that objective was to go after convention bookings. Conventions are one of the less charming aspects of twentieth-century travel, although they do help sustain the hotels, the whiskey industry, and the local merchants and restaurants. Conventioneers have a way of disturbing the peace of mind of any nonconvention guests, as well as damaging and destroying the carpets and furnishings.

Convention business is an essential to any large-size hotel; it's a way of hedging the bets. Only a relatively small hotel can afford to ignore it and to cater strictly to the independent, luxury-demanding patron. In the United States, there are a handful of such hotels: in Boston, the Ritz; in New York, the Pierre, Carlyle, and the Waldorf Towers; in Chicago, the Ritz; in San Francisco, the Stanford Court; in Beverly Hills, the Beverly Wilshire and the Bel-Air. In London, there are Claridge's, the Connaught, the Savoy, and the Berkeley; in Paris, the Plaza-Athenée, the Bristol, and the worn-at-the-seams Ritz; in Zurich, the Baur-au-Lac and the Dolder Grand; in Vienna, the Imperial; in Rome, the Grand; in Venice, the Gritti-Palace; in Hong Kong, the Peninsula; and in Tokyo, the Okura.

The hotels I have specifically mentioned provide all of the amenities of superb and gracious service, excellent room maintenance, fine housekeeping, interested management supervision, and top-quality cuisine—and they charge for it! There are many other hotels which make claim to luxury service and may even have deluxe ratings in the guides, but they fail to measure up in one way or another. Great hotels don't become great by chance; they achieve greatness because a great manager, by hard work, establishes and maintains standards of quality for everything—from the freshness of the oysters to the manners of the telephone operators, from the laundry service to the wine selection.

He must be a good leader of people with the ability to infuse his staff with the principles of his own operating philosophy, but he must also possess many of the skills of a professional diplomat, for situations develop in hotel operation requiring both imaginative solutions and judicious decisions. When Henri J. P. Manassero, now managing director of the Hotel Pierre in New York, was at the Carlton in Cannes, as a trainee manager, word came from the Egyptian embassy in Paris that King Farouk wanted to visit Cannes a week hence for the month of July, and would require the entire top floor of the hotel for himself and attendants. This was at the height of the season, and the Carlton was not only completely filled but was booked up for the following four weeks.

Many regular guests occupied quarters on the top floor, and they had to be induced to move to other rooms; cables were sent to those holding reservations, explaining that a crisis had occurred and asking for a delay in arrival or acceptance of reservations at other hotels. Within twenty-four hours they had cleared the top floor to accommodate the king of Egypt; and, by skillful negotiations, supplemented, no doubt, by magnums of champagne and bottles of perfume, had rearranged the accommodations of some forty other guests in a manner that caused no lasting enmities for the Carlton.

VIP's can be exasperating when they use their wealth to circumvent standard operating policies and demand special privileges. Max Blouet, the longtime manager of the George V in Paris, cited Paul Getty, then regarded as the world's wealthiest individual, as the most difficult and trying guest in his hotel-management career. Mr. Getty called Blouet one day after Christmas and told him he had a problem, for he had received a gift of two cases of magnums of champagne. Blouet replied, "Mr. Getty, that's no problem. You should feel happy that someone wanted to honor you with such a handsome gift." "But," replied Mr. Getty, "I don't like to open a magnum when I have just six guests. Could you do me a favor and exchange them for quarts?" Blouet said he

Search for the Best: Bed and Board

95

would be happy to make the swap, even though his wine steward objected because magnums were harder to sell. A few days later, Mr. Getty called back and said, "Mr. Blouet, you were nice to help me out when you traded the magnums for quarts, but I hate to open the quarts for just a few friends. Would you mind changing them for splits?"

Some time later, Mr. Getty approached Blouet, asking him for a reduction on his bill as a professional courtesy, since he owned the Pierre Hotel in New York and the Pierre Marques in Acapulco. It was not the matter of money, he said, but just one of principle. Blouet promised to study the matter and to advise him of the decision at a later time.

He went immediately to his accounting department and gave instructions that Mr. Getty was to be the hotel's guest for the rental of the apartment and food for one week. I asked Blouet if he wasn't taking a big chance that Getty would run up a staggering bill. "No," he said, "I wasn't risking too much, for Mr. Getty was very careful about his expenditures, and I left him unaware of the special arrangement regarding his bill during the whole week. After he received his bill, he was very pleased; but he could *not* ask us anything else in the weeks and weeks to come, during which he stayed at the George V!"

Hernando Courtright, now the innkeeper emeritus of the Beverly Wilshire Hotel, was a vice-president of the Bank of America during the Depression, when he was sent out to operate the Beverly Hills Hotel after the bank foreclosed its mortgage. He liked the hotel business so much that he found a few friends to help him buy the property. Even before he redecorated the rooms, he trained his staff to address the guests by name—at the front desk, on the telephone, by the room-service operator, by the bellmen. Visitors were captivated by this personalized service and, although they recognized it as sophisticated sales promotion, they liked it and kept coming back.

When Courtright left the Beverly Hills Hotel to buy the Beverly Wilshire Hotel, he carried the same technique there, where it worked equally well. One of his past lieutenants remarked, "In Courtright's hotel, service is the name of the game, the guest is a god!" I think this is a worthy evaluation, but I wish that he would recognize that although gods may have lights in the middle of their foreheads, ordinary mortals depend on lamps at night; although the rooms do have lamps, they are more decorative than illuminating.

Bernard Shaw wrote in "Maxims for Revolutionists" in *Man and Superman:* "The reasonable man adapts himself to the world: the unreasonable one persists in trying to adapt the world to himself. Therefore all progress depends on the unreasonable man."

The conditions prevailing in the hotel industry in the mid-1960s made an unreasonable man out of James Nassikas, a young hotel operator who had obtained his B.S. degree in hotel management at the University of New Hampshire and an advanced degree at L'Ecole Hôtelière in Lausanne. He worked for the Sonnabend chain at the Mayflower in Washington and at the Plaza in New York before getting the assignment to assist in the conceptualization and building of the Royal Orleans Hotel in New Orleans' Vieux Carré in 1957, which he managed after its completion.

In addition to being a well-schooled, practical hotel operator, Nassikas was unreasonable enough to understand how great hotels could be and how poor they turned out to be; he had the ambition to overcome the economic forces responsible for the current state of hotel mediocrity and to build a hotel of great distinction. His analysis coincided with that of William B. Tabler, an architect who had specialized in hotel design in the mid-1940s.

In 1971, Tabler made a speech that was quoted in an article appearing in the *Lodging and Food Service News,* in which he said that hotels of today are at least twenty years or more old the day they are opened and "can never become great and famous," and that, "up until 1955, architects' hotel clients were pioneering, strong-willed, visionary men such as Ellsworth Statler, Conrad Hilton, and Ernest Henderson. The result was a kind of person-to-person relationship between the architect and hotel man in which innovation and excellence prospered, and a great many new things were introduced." He added that "It would be difficult to name any innovations of similar importance that have appeared in hotel design

Search for the Best: Bed and Board

since then; the few innovations in the industry are being developed, not by hotel men, but by the small motel owner-operators."

He went on to explain that the reason for this change is that the architect seldom sees the client anymore, and oftentimes doesn't even know who he is. "Hotels," Tabler said, "are now built and approved by committees; and committees don't take risks. All committees can do is check out and approve what has been successful in the past and repeat it." A large hotel-chain operating company provides its know-how to manage a hotel on a contract basis for a fee and looks to the developer to put up the money. This condition provides many bosses for the architect who must give approval, with the result that time runs out, and the only thing that can be done to meet completion schedules is to plan the next hotel like the last one built. "It will be all right, but it won't be great. . . ."

Tabler's description of the economic forces influencing hotel architecture apply with equal cogency to store buildings and office structures alike. Of course, there is the exceptional client, like Seagram, which engaged Mies van der Rohe to design the Seagram Building in New York City, and Gerald Hines of Houston, who commissioned Philip Johnson to do the dazzlingly beautiful Pennzoil Building in Houston. But, for every exception, there are thousands of dull, uninspired architectural repetitions, many of which show the obvious signs of having been designed by a committee rather than a client. Folklore has it that the camel was the result of compromises made by a committee during the time of creation.

Nassikas had become close friends with Edgar B. Stern, Jr., whose family owned the Royal Orleans, and to whom he confided his dream about the hotel he hoped to build and run someday. He conceptualized a hotel with a sense of place, where his guests could look around and know they were not in Kansas City or Atlanta, where there was a sense of human scale in the design that would beneficially affect both guests and staff, where the normal clichés of hotel furnishings would be scrupulously avoided.

These were the dreams of Mr. Nassikas. After Mr. Stern heard and digested them, he turned to his dreamer friend, and said, "Let's do one all alone someday." That someday came when an old apartment hotel in San Francisco became available. It was gutted and completely rebuilt into today's Stanford Court, one of the most charming fine-quality hotels in the entire country. Only an unreasonable man like its president, Mr. Nassikas, could have accomplished it.

One of the attributes of a deluxe hotel is a fine kitchen, but the great restaurants of the world are, for the most part, independent of hotel affiliations. Invariably, their greatness is the reflection of the owner, whether he be the chef or the maître'd'hôtel. The preparation of fine food, like all other productions, is an exacting business, permitting no room for shortcuts or compromises.

If my thesis that bigness is inimical to fine quality is valid, then it is doubly true in cooking, for the chef must be able to keep his eye on each and every dish being prepared by his *sous-chefs*, to be able to taste the sauce, to test the tenderness of the meat, to smell the bouquet of the soup. His refrigerators must be large enough for a varied menu and small enough to limit his reserves to a one-day supply. He must have a team of specialists whom he supervises with the mastermind of a football coach as he mentally recalls every dish in preparation on the range. He cooks with his head.

Most of the famous chefs of France are male chauvinists in their conviction that only men make great restaurant chefs, dismissing women's abilities with the quotation of Curnonsky, "A woman cooks as a bird sings"—for love and not commerce. They contend that a man cooks for himself, out of pride, and as a means of self-expression. It is not surprising that the late Helen Corbitt, under whose direction the Neiman-Marcus Zodiac restaurants became famous, disagreed.

Normally, fine food calls for fine presentation. Great chefs are proud of the way they send their platters to the table. Soulé at Le Pavillon used Baccarat crystal stemware, Masson at La Grenouille dressed his dining rooms with huge bouquets of fresh flowers, Helen Corbitt exercised color control in the combination of vegetables that were served. Raymond Oliver at Le Grand Vefour in Paris revived the use of eighteenth-century compotes for table service. In the best of restaurants, the headwaiters have an intimate knowledge of the market availability, so that they don't recommend things that aren't fresh or good enough to be bought that day.

If I had to name a single restaurant where I would have to eat every meal for a whole month, it would unquestionably be Harry's Bar in Venice. The greatness of its food is in its simplicity; I leave satisfied, but never full. The variety offered by its menu would do credit to any restaurant located in Paris or New York, but the best sources of information about the offerings of the day are the waiters, whose recommendations are infallible. They are warm and friendly and insistent to please, and they are not averse to disagreeing with a guest as to what he should order. One evening, I asked our waiter to bring some bread and butter. "No," he said, "it will spoil your appetite." Harry's Bar is small, crowded, and noisy, but its food has that badly maligned quality of tasting like it was in the golden age of home-cooking.

Fine restaurants are staffed with an ample number of waiters and busboys, so that glasses are kept filled, bread and butter constantly resupplied, plates promptly removed. Their prices are high, as they must be for all of the skills and services employed in such an establishment.

In better restaurants, particularly, there is keen competition for the tables which are considered best. Obviously a table located next to a service station or adjacent to the kitchen door is not a good one, and a banquette for two is better than a freestanding table, but those considerations aside, all other tables are of about equal quality in fact. The truth is, however, that certain tables or sections of rooms in most restaurants have acquired a social status, either by accident or design. "21" in New York has been cursed by its back room, which it brought on itself, by relegating to that area nonestablishment and unknown out-of-town patrons. As a result, the room has a stigma which no regular customer will accept, however hungry he might be. Mike Romanoff tried to solve the problem by designing a circular dining room, where there could be no favored corner because there were no corners. His best customers decided otherwise, deciding that the north side was better than the opposite side. At the Four Seasons, it's a table around the pool; at Chasen's, it's a booth; at La Grenouille and La Côte Basque, it's the front section of banquettes. The food is identical in any location in a restaurant, but it doesn't taste the same.

Whenever I visit a restaurant for the first time in the United States, I usually test its quality by ordering a crabmeat cocktail and an omelet. If they have lump crab on the menu as an appetizer, I am curious to know whether it is fresh, and if it is indeed lump crab meat and not Alaskan crab, and if it is served with too large a bed of lettuce and cut-up celery. If it is neither fresh nor lump crab, nor generous in its serving, I return it and I'll never go back, for I know then that the restaurant is just a second-rater. A good omelet is simple to make, but rarely is it done masterfully. There's no sauce to hide its imperfections. As a matter of fact, when an experienced restaurateur tests a chef applicant, he asks him to make an omelet or a *sauce normande*, both of which have to be done with speed and skill, for once started there's no turning back. In a way, this test is like painting a watercolor, in which every stroke of the brush leaves its mark, not to be corrected at a later stage by painting over.

A restaurant guest should never be hesitant about sending back a tough piece of meat, over- or undercooked vegetables or fowl, or a bottle of wine that is corky or over the hill, but he should do so only if his knowledge about food and wines makes him a qualified critic. He does the restaurant owner a favor when he does so, particularly if his complaint is registered in a quiet and dignified manner.

The United States is the home of mass-produced, popular food—the hot dog, the hamburger, the doughnut—quick-food operations offering a wide variety of food specialties from pizzas to frozen yogurt; it maintains sanitary conditions in the kitchens as good or better than any other place in the world.

There are many good restaurants in France, the United States, Switzerland, Italy, England, and Belgium. There are a limited number of great restaurants in the world, with most of them concentrated in France, many in New York, and one in Italy. There are thousands of mediocre pretentious restaurants all over the world, with a high percentage of them located within our continental boundaries.

The food business has suffered badly from the effects of mass production and it will probably never recover. The loss of the apprentice system and the failure to develop substitute methods for teaching the various skills in food preparation and service are irreparable. Diners aren't eating as well and won't eat as well as they did fifty years ago. The only culinary pluses from the Industrial Revolution have been refrigeration and rapid transportation, but the minuses are quick-frozen foods and the microwave oven, chemically fed fowl and livestock.

Mass production has hit the restaurant industry as well as others. For the sake of economy many restaurants serve "homemade" beef stew which is canned in Chicago, stuffed flounder prepared and frozen by large processors in Philadelphia, roast beef presliced and quick-frozen in New York, and tasteless, nutritionless vegetables frozen in all parts of the world. Fowl and livestock fed on a chemically enriched diet or from chemically fertilized crops have different and less desirable physical characteristics, including texture and taste.

Thomas Whiteside wrote a devastating essay in *The New Yorker* that might have been titled "Recollections of Things Past," things past being the vine-ripened tomato. His account of the development of a tomato with uniformity of size to facilitate machine picking, thickness of skin to improve shelf-life, and the ethylene-gassing of green tomatoes to turn them red—all at the expense of taste and flavor—gives further documentation to mass production's effect on quality. May Ceres, goddess of the harvests, protect peaches, mangoes, raspberries, and all of the other virginal fruits which, until now, come to market tree- or vine-ripened.

The French are credited with having invented sauces to disguise the flavor and smell of fowl and fish and meat that were past their prime. Today, restaurants are using sauces with equal volume to give flavor to the tasteless, frozen fowl and fish and meat. *"Plus ça change, plus c'est la même chose."*

The number of eating facilities has so boomed in recent years that eateries of one sort or another virtually surround us. This fact notwithstanding, it is difficult to find a first-quality, unadulterated hamburger, a nongreasy piece of fried chicken, a slice of pie that tastes as if it came from a kitchen rather than a factory.

Food is big business in the United States and the mass producers and distributors have put profit into it even as they have taken it out. This unhappy result comes, in part, from catering to a mass market in which the taste factor is lowered to satisfy the greatest number of customers, and in part from economic pressures that encourage some of the hamburger-makers to stretch their product by adding foreign, less costly ingredients, such as cereals. I don't mean to infer that it is impossible to get good hamburgers in this country, but you have to work hard to find them.

Chain-hotel food, supervised by profit-conscious Cornell and Michigan State hotel-school graduates, has become as standardized, banal, and tasteless as that served by most of the airlines. Having operated a money-losing restaurant business at Neiman-Marcus for many years, I am most appreciative of the need for efficiency and profit, but I refuse to believe that it's necessary to serve poor, unimaginative food to accomplish those objectives. If steaks are too expensive to be profitable, then prepare the best beef stew; if crab is too costly, then serve mussels in a mustard mayonnaise, or tuna salad.

If we can judge American taste in food by the huge tonnage of cookbooks sold annually, by the vast interest in the cookware departments, and by the demand for gourmet foods in the epicure shops, then the mass-food industry has missed the general public's desire for food with new taste and flavor sensations.

With the exception of New York, most American cities have relatively few, if any, general restaurants that could be regarded as first-rate by domestic or international standards, with all due respect to the *Holiday* magazine awards and the *Mobil Travel Guide*'s grading system. If Michelin were to operate in this country, its printer would need very few stars in his type box. There are specialty restaurants all over the country that are great for single dishes, like Angelo's in Fort Worth for barbecue, Joe's in Miami for stone crabs, and the Oyster Bar in Grand Central Terminal in New York City. Would that there were more restaurants doing one thing superbly well, using where possible the local products!

The three greatest gourmet food emporia in the world, I would suggest, are Fauchon in Paris, Fortnum & Mason, and Harrods Food Hall in London. All three of them deal in both the staples and exotic products of all lands, but I find that my salivary glands are more stimulated as I walk through Fauchon than the other two. At Fortnum's, I get the impression that its customers are buying gifts; at Harrods', I find the crowds distracting; but at Fauchon, I feel that I am in the midst of a group of people who like to eat and have come there because they know they'll find what they are looking for as well as a number of delicacies they never knew existed. This is a personal preference, and I yield to those who differ in this evaluation.

Fauchon, located on the place de la Madeleine in Paris, was operated by Edmond Bory, who bought the bankrupt business in 1953 and catapulted the name into fame by bringing to his store delicacies from all over the world—wherever Air France flew. Thus, the shopper will find melons from Spain, limes from Brazil, giant strawberries from Japan, Chinese gooseberries from New Zealand, cherries from Chile, and maple syrup from Vermont. In addition to twenty-four kinds of mustard, sixteen types of honey, and fifty-two varieties of tea, the shelves are full of Kellogg's corn flakes, chili beans from Gebhardt's of San Antonio, Aunt Jemima pancake mix. Naturally, caviar is available in great supply, as it is at Fortnum's and Harrods', but *tapinade*, the chopped-olive relish of Provence, can be bought there as well and not at either of the English stores.

Fauchon has an extensive wine and liquor department, and a section of *gastronomie* where prepared fowl, salads, roasts, and fish can be purchased for home consumption. Near the main store is the candy and pastry shop and a stand-up food bar that provides deluxe quick luncheons to an endless number of people.

The prepared foods, pastries, and candies are made in Fauchon's kitchens; the canned and bottled goods are packed for them under their own label by the best processors Bory can locate. He has a fine sense of packaging and presentation which has enabled him to market his nonperishable luxury food products to select stores around the world. He is a man of sure personal taste in the broad sense of the word, but he employs several professional tasters to test the actual merchandise he buys and sells. Like other successful quality entrepreneurs, he loves his business and, although he is a great innovator, he is persistent in his fidelity to his concept: "My job is to teach, to point the way. The purpose of a store like this is to establish standards of taste and then to defend them. I don't sell food; I sell quality."

Habit de Paticier

A Paris, Chez N. de Larmessin, Rüe S. Jacques, à la Pomie d'Or,   Avec Privil. du Roy

7

Search for the Best:
Taste and Smell

There is not a diet book I know in which any of the delicacies I'm going to discuss are mentioned, for they are on the *Index Alimentum Prohibitum* issued by the Puritans of our day, the medicine men who have discovered that almost everything we eat is bad for us. The more delectable the food, the more certain it is to have those qualities which will increase our cholesterol or our triglyceride fats. Even if we ignore their warnings, they have succeeded in spoiling the enjoyment of the food by their scientific pronouncements—for the first bite, at least. Only two delicious foods have escaped their prohibited list to date, grapefruit and cantaloupe. They are both so good that I think it's simply a matter of time before the professionals will declare them to be harmful.

Every geographical region has its own homegrown delicacies that are esteemed by its residents. Some have local acceptance, others are internationally appreciated; some are in short supply, others are relatively abundant. The best qualities of all of them are expensive. From the world's larder of superdelicacies, I have chosen to investigate a few of them which have the greatest international acceptance, namely, caviar, smoked salmon, *foie gras*, chocolate, and ice cream.

The best-known product of Russia is unknown there by the name we call it, "caviar." To them it is *ikra*, and they relish it just as much as we do. The English name for the roe of the Caspian sturgeon is derived from the Turkish word *havyar,* but whether you call it "caviar" or "*ikra,*" it is the most expensive food product in the world, with the finest quality retailing, as of this writing, at $175 for a fourteen-ounce tin.

Even Shakespeare was aware of caviar, for in *Hamlet,* Act II, Hamlet says, ". . . for the play, I remember, pleased not the million; 'twas caviare to the general," meaning, it was like caviar, esteemed by the epicures, but repugnant to the general public. The enjoyment of caviar may be a cultivated taste, but times have changed since Shakespeare, and in the twentieth century it doesn't require much cultivation. A masterpiece of understatement appeared in Savary's *Dictionnaire du Commerce* (1741), on the subject of caviar: "It is beginning to be known in France where it is not despised at the best tables."

The sturgeons are found in many waters, including the Hudson and Mississippi rivers, some waterways in Canada, and in the Azov Sea in Russia; but the place where they abound in greatest number is the Caspian Sea, fed by rivers in Iran and the Volga in Russia. Many have been the arguments I've heard about the relative merits of Iranian and Russian caviar, but my research shows that the sturgeons are ideologically nonpolitical and that the roe taken from them on both sides of the Caspian are of equal quality. Water pollution could be a factor that might affect the catch on either side, but there is little authoritative information on this aspect of the subject. The methods of handling, grading, salting, and packing the roe may vary slightly, but I question if there are caviar testers who can identify the national origin of caviar from the Caspian.

The Beluga sturgeon, often weighing up to twenty-five hundred pounds, provides the largest eggs. The membrane holding the roe is broken and the eggs are passed through screens for grading purposes. Then, one pound of salt is added to each *pud* (a Russian weight, roughly equivalent to forty-one American pounds) which transforms the raw roe into edible caviar. This small amount of salt is described in Russian as *malosol,* meaning "little salt." When properly graded and salted, the caviar is then put into tins or jars and labeled "Beluga Malosol." However, there are two characteristics that are even more important criteria of quality than the size of the egg. The first is that the egg must be uncrushed and whole; the second is that the egg must be well covered with its own natural shining fat. For the latter reason, the caviar tins should be turned over at regular intervals to keep the fatty ingredient evenly distributed. All nonpasteurized caviar must be kept under constant refrigeration, but under no condition should it ever be frozen, for once frozen and thawed, the eggs will burst. The smaller eggs are lightly compressed into tins or jars with the addition of salt and are marketed under the trade term of "pressed caviar." This product was described by one of the great caviar authorities, the late General Malcolm K. Beyer, as "resembling in its final state a gooey mass similar to a thick marmalade," and is favored by some connoisseurs to the whole-grain variety. Above all, caviar should have no fishy smell; any fish odor is an indication there has been some tampering in an effort to raise the grade.

The variety of sturgeon producing eggs second in size to the Beluga is the Ossetra, or Ossetrina, also called Ossetrova. The smallest egg is produced by the Sevruga sturgeon, also spelled Sevriouga and Chivrouga. The quality of these, as well as of the Beluga, depends on the handling of the roe and the amount of salt added. The smaller eggs command a lower market price than the larger eggs of the Beluga.

Where does all the caviar go? A lot of it stays at home, for there is a large domestic consumption in Russia; no comparable figures for Iran are available. France is the largest importer of caviar from both Russia and Iran, with Germany and the United States running neck and neck for second place. The balance is distributed to the rest of the non-Muslim world —wherever there is a sufficiently wealthy market to buy at ever-increasing prices. Since 1960, prices have soared from $35 for fourteen ounces to the current price, with little or no effect on demand. People with money and a taste for caviar are willing to pay the price.

Now to the eating! There are numerous ways of serving caviar and each has its proponents. Some like it with a garnishment of chopped egg whites and yolks, minced parsley, and onions. I suspect this was devised by an ingenious chef to camouflage an inferior grade of caviar. The Russians made use of *blini,* their traditional pancakes, upon which the caviar is heaped and covered with sour cream. Since the *blini* are bland, they act as a perfect foil for the distinctive flavor of caviar. In Poland, a split baked potato is served similarly as a neutral receptacle for caviar, topped with sour cream. If the caviar is of the best quality, my own preference is to put it on a piece of melba toast, without butter, for there is sufficient fat in the caviar to make butter unnecessary. Lemon should be used sparingly and only on the more heavily salted variety. I must admit that my very favorite unsocial way of eating caviar is by the spoonful, *au naturel.*

———

Less expensive, but still costly, is the other fish delicacy, smoked salmon. At London clubs, French and American restaurants, or wherever smoked salmon is available, it is a most popular appetizer. The salmon is a fish of the Northern Hemisphere that lives in salt water and spawns in fresh water, though some species are landlocked in lakes. Each region in which salmon swim proclaims the superior virtues of its local catch, but for the purpose of smoking, it is generally considered that Scotland produces the best fish. Most fine restaurants list "Smoked Scotch Salmon," though at times they may substitute Norwegian or Irish salmon, either through necessity or ignorance. When you eat smoked salmon in London, it is likely that the fish has been smoked in London rather than in Scotland, but it's still called smoked Scotch salmon. The London smokers use more salt, which seems to suit the British taste better. In Scotland, they treat the fish with salt and then with a coating of molasses to give their salmon a slightly sweeter flavor.

The demand for smoked Scotch salmon is so great that the Scotch smokers sometimes import fish from Nova Scotia, where the salmon is similar to theirs. Some American sellers even ship Nova Scotia salmon to Scotland to be smoked and then reshipped to the United States, claiming they get a better product than when the fish is smoked in Nova Scotia. In such cases, the fish should be labeled "Scotch-smoked salmon" rather than "smoked Scotch salmon."

The best Scotch salmon is firm and not mushy, and its color may range from the tender pink of the dawn's sky to the pinkish-orange of a Texas sunset. Whenever you are served Scotch salmon with a deep orange color, reject it, for it is either not fresh or it has been overtreated in the smoking process. Nova Scotia salmon is darker than its Scotch counterpart, and it will be more orange and have a stronger flavor. When you see a bright-red blood mark in the salmon meat, either send it back or cut around it, for that indicates the mark where the salmon was gaffed.

Some restaurants serve capers and chopped onions with the salmon, but since the best smoked salmon has such a delicate flavor, these additives are too competitive. In my opinion, fresh-ground pepper is the only supplement needed. (Speaking of pepper reminds me that the best pepper mills are produced by Peugeot, the French automobile maker. They are far superior to and more durable than any other on the market. Peugeot markets them with wood bodies, but also sells the stainless-steel mechanism to other manufacturers who encase them in glass, pewter, and other materials.)

Much richer and more filling as an appetizer is *foie gras;* as a matter of fact, it is a meal in itself. A goose *foie gras* should not be confused with a *pâté de foie gras* any more than a sirloin steak should be classified with a meat loaf. A *pâté* may contain some goose liver mixed with a forcemeat of pork, bacon, and seasoning, but a goose *foie gras* is the whole liver whose gargantuan size results from forced feeding of the fowl. "The goose," says C. Gérard, author of *L'Ancienne Alsace à Table,* "is nothing, but man has made it an instrument for the output of a marvelous product, a living hothouse in which grows the supreme fruit of gastronomy." It is certainly one of the greatest delicacies available for those with good digestive powers.

The provinces of Landes, Périgord, and Alsace are the three main centers for goose-raising in France, but it is doubtful if

Search for the Best: Taste and Smell

all three could produce the quantity of goose livers to fill the crocks of *foie gras* and *pâté de foie gras* shipped annually from France. It is reported that one of Hungary's largest exports is the shipment of goose livers to France. *Foie gras* packed in Hungary, when available, is as fine as you can get; sliced and served cold on hot toast, it is a superb appetizer. One of the most memorable dishes I have ever eaten was hot, fresh goose liver cooked in white wine with seeded green grapes at the Jockey Club in Madrid, but I have never seen it on any menu since then. Just thinking about *foie gras* jumps my cholesterol.

Montezuma never had the pleasure of eating goose *foie gras*, for geese weren't native to his land, but the Spanish conquistadores were quick to observe that he drank fifty cups of *chocolatl* a day. The Spaniards took the cocoa bean home with them, and introduced the sweetened drink to the court, where it met with great acceptance. Cortes, having had the foresight to plant cocoa beans in Trinidad, Haiti, and the African island Fernando Po, gave Spain a monopoly in chocolate that lasted until the eighteenth century. Eating-chocolate was a product of the mid-nineteenth century, when it was marketed in London by Fry and Sons, and then given further impetus through the development of milk chocolate by Nestlé in Switzerland in 1876.

The invention of the steam engine came about almost simultaneously, making it possible to use steam power to drive roasters, grinders, mixers, and chocolate presses. Thus, chocolate-candy manufacturing, almost from its beginning, became one of the first industries to experience the effects of the Industrial Revolution. There are three basic kinds of chocolate candy: first, the homemade or candy-kitchen type, made with fresh cream and butter for fast consumption; second, a product manufactured for wide distribution, requiring additives to insure a long shelf-life; and third, a machine-made candy using only fresh ingredients and which is shipped by air to its customers to assure freshness even with the absence of preservatives.

My memory goes back to the 1920s, when Maillard was the foremost candymaker in the United States, and admittedly, nostalgia may be warping my judgment, but I think that company made the finest chocolate candy ever made in this country or in the world. They no longer make bonbons, only cooking chocolate, candy bars, and a few specialty items. Mirror's, in New York, was a fine candy store, with a specialty of a chocolate-covered molasses chip which has never since been equaled. Bissinger's of Cincinnati and, later, St. Louis made top-quality chocolates and gained fame for their chocolate-covered fondant with a whole pecan in the middle. There were, and still are, scores of small candymakers producing limited quantities of fine chocolate for their local clienteles.

The mass-produced candy is so good and so relatively inexpensive that many candy eaters have never felt the need to try the more expensive kind. Automation has provided the consumers with a superb value, and candymaking in general is one of the best examples of the benefits resultant from the mass-production system. The handmade segment of the industry is suffering from the same problems faced by all other manufacturers requiring hand labor.

Michael and Ariane Batterberry commented in their interesting piece in *New York* magazine, "Today the local purveyor of freshly hand-dipped chocolate is an endangered species, simply because the dippers, like lace workers and master piano-tuners, are themselves a vanishing breed." Godiva, of Belgium, was the first to employ this method, until the makers of Campbell Soup bought the company and started producing the candy in Connecticut. Neuhaus of Belgium ships by air to Neiman-Marcus, and Le Nôtre of Paris services Marshall Field in the same manner.

With the exception of a few-odd specialty pieces, I prefer American- and Belgian-made chocolate candies to those made in other countries. Each geographical area has its own taste as to sweetness versus bitterness and its preferences between cream-filled, caramels, marshmallows, molasses chips, and a score of others. I happen to like both the Belgian chocolate flavor and the general assortment of pieces. I consider Godiva the best candy made in the United States, despite a lack of innovation. Even though Godiva uses the same formulas and the same methods as when it was originally made in Belgium, the American Godiva candy has a different flavor, due doubtlessly to the different characteristics of Belgian and U.S. cream and butter. Of the several made-in-Belgium chocolates, I find Neuhaus the best. Krön Chocolatier makes a fine candy, which pleases by its witty design as well as by its superb quality and unique flavor. The best marshmallows are made by Schwartz on West Seventy-second Street in New York City.

The specialty pieces to which I referred are the *truffes* of Fauchon; the peppermint-chocolate wafer of Cova of Milan, which I like better than the similar but not quite so refined item made by Bendicks of England; and, finally, the greatest single piece of candy in the world, the *carrées*, a chocolate sandwich one-eighth of an inch thick with fruit-flavored fillings, made by Sprüngli of Zurich.

Chocolate-manufacturing and ice-cream–making came of age at about the same time, in the middle of the nineteenth century, but it seems to me that chocolate has suffered less damage from the effects of mass production than ice cream. With few exceptions the ice cream we eat today has only a faint resemblance to the ice cream Mother used to make at home; it may be healthier with its lowered butterfat content, but it doesn't taste as good. Ice cream just isn't what it used to be—despite the fact that it is still cold and sweet. Thereafter, any resemblance ceases.

Homemade ice cream had numerous recipes, but they all were based on the use of cream or milk, or a combination of both, with or without egg yolks. Economic and market forces brought about changes in the formula that is used in today's commercial ice cream. Rising costs of dairy products forced the reduction of the amount of cream used and the inclusion of other ingredients to compensate for the loss of the qualities that the high butterfat provided. Stabilizers in the form of gelatin or other products were added to prevent the formation of ice crystals caused by the reduction of cream. Emulsifiers, the other additives, make the ice cream smoother and more whippable through the introduction of a greater amount of air to the mix, thus inflating the volume of ice cream being produced. Government regulations require a minimum of 10 percent butterfat, giving assurance that at least a little cream will still be used in the making of ice cream. This compares with the 16 percent to 18 percent butterfat of some of the great ice creams of the past, such as those formerly made by Louis Sherry, Wil Wright, and Howard Johnson, *et al.*

The drive for cost control brought about both the reduction of the amount of cream used and the development of ice-cream–making machinery. The marketing people in the industry contend that the low butterfat product, which is less rich and filling, has encouraged larger consumption. Certainly it has a lower cholesterol content and fewer calories. Wil Wright once told me that the only way to make an old-fashioned ice cream was by using old-fashioned ice-cream–making equipment, for the high butterfat content clogged up the new, high-speed machinery. When I reproved him for giving away his famous recipes to competition, he replied, "When they find out how expensive it is to make my ice cream, they won't copy it."

Bassetts in Philadelphia still makes the kind of ice cream which made it famous; most of the others have succumbed to the new method. If you want the finest ice cream in the world, then you will have to go to Florence, to the Via Isola d'elle Stinche, and visit Vivoli, a little ice-cream shop located behind the church of Santa Croce, where a wide variety of flavors are served in paper cups of varying sizes. You can order one flavor or a variety of four ice creams or a mixture of ice creams and water ices. The tart lemon ice and the ice creams have no competition anywhere. As you wind your way through the narrow Florentine streets toward Vivoli's you will pick up a trail of paper cups, and as they increase in quantity, you will know that you are getting closer to your goal. Vivoli is open from 8:30 to 12:30 A.M., Tuesday through Saturday. Sunday hours are 10:00 A.M. to 1:00 P.M. and 4:00 P.M. to 12:30 A.M. At opening hour on Sunday, after the siesta, you will find a clamoring mob of several hundred waiting for the iron shutters to roll up. Don't worry, they never run out.

"Mr. Armand Petitjean of Lancôme is on the phone," my secretary said. "He has just heard you were in Paris and wants to invite you to luncheon next Tuesday at Lucas-Carton on the place de la Madeleine." Mr. Petitjean had the reputation for being one of the best-informed perfumers in France, and incidentally, for being a great gourmet, so I accepted with alacrity. I knew that he was trying to woo me to take on the Lancôme line for the store, which did not interest us at the time, but I was only too glad to have this opportunity of learning more about the perfume industry from one of the great noses of France. Mr. Petitjean had risen to a top position at Coty and then left to found the Lancôme cosmetic and perfume business. After a superb meal, including fresh truffles, we got around to the subject of perfume and the various elements that affect its quality. He explained that modern technology made perfume a better product than it ever had been in the past, and that all of the leading perfumers were capable of making perfumes of comparable quality. The main difference between them, he said, was in their ability to anticipate taste changes in fragrances and to be leaders rather than followers. The great houses of Houbigant and Coty of the early part of the century had lost their positions of supremacy because they thought that Quelques Fleurs and Idéal (Houbigant) and L'Origan (Coty) were here to stay forever.

They were duly shocked, after World War I, when the dressmaker Chanel developed a fragrance and brought it to market under the name Chanel No. 5. It became a raging success. For the first time, a new chemical component, an aldehyde, was used to give the perfume a bright, new top-note, and it rode to fame on Chanel's own couture success and the publicity she organized for it. She was joined a few years later in 1927 by another *couturière*, Jeanne Lanvin, who introduced another trendsetter, Arpège. Both of these perfumes were based on light, blended floral bouquets.

Houbigant and Coty retrieved their standing; but Guerlain,

another old-line perfumer, who had contributed a trend fragrance in 1898 with a heavy Oriental perfume called Jicky, rallied and continued to bring out fragrances which were influential, such as the mossy-bouquet Mitsouko in 1921 and the Oriental Shalimar in 1925. Mitsouko was the forerunner of later perfumes like Ma Griffe of Carven, Calèche by Hermès, Y by Yves Saint Laurent, and Calandre by Paco Rabanne. Shalimar, with its vanilla-rose-jasmine complex set the stage for Tabu by Dana, Shocking by Schiaparelli, and Bal à Versailles by Jean Desprez.

Jean Patou brought out Joy, a straight jasmine fragrance, and it was a leader, as was also Femme by Marcel Rochas in 1942. The latter used a fruit aldehyde, previously introduced by Guerlain in Vague Souvenir without success. Thus ended Mr. Petitjean's analysis, which I later had corroborated by my old friends Gregory Thomas and Dick Salomon, formerly heads, respectively, of Chanel U.S.A. and Lanvin-Charles of the Ritz.

The first fine-quality perfume made in the United States to achieve any stature was White Shoulders, by Evyan, introduced in 1936 by Dr. Walter Langer, an Austrian immigrant. He was a scientist, doing research in metals, until he received an assignment to work in essential oils. With the knowledge he gained in this field, he decided he had learned enough to create his own perfume. It was an erotic blend of the oils of the flower of the ilang-ilang tree, the tuberose, and the magnolia blossom. It became a trendsetter, paving the way for the similar but greatly intensified Youth Dew of Estée Lauder in 1952.

For several centuries the fragrance business has been a French monopoly, since most of the essential floral oils emanated from Grasse, on the Riviera. After the war, some of the French companies set up plants in the United States to service the volume fragrance distributors like Avon, and the large soap producers. There was a time when a perfume not made and bottled in France bore such a stigma that no fine-quality store would offer it for sale. About ten years ago, Charles Revson launched Norell, conceived and made in America. It was a new and great fragrance and it became a tremendous hit.

That marked the beginning of the American revolution in the perfume industry and the breaking of the French monopoly. Today, the United States has about 65 percent of the home market and about 35 percent of European fragrance sales. Revlon followed up its initial success very quickly with Charlie, backing it with a $10-million introductory campaign, and made it the world's best-selling fragrance. The Norton Simon conglomerate bought Halston's apparel business and brought out a perfume, Halston, at $65 an ounce with similar financial promotion, and it too has proved to be a great success. The U.S. manufacturers adopted the French technique of using designer names, but they have added the American know-how of market research, together with heavy advertising budget and gifts-with-purchase.

If we dismiss the matter of trend setting, for the moment, and consider two new fragrances within an existing trend that come on the market at the same time, what is the factor that may make one commercially successful and the other a failure? Very obviously, the acceptance factor will be influenced by which has the greatest amount and best quality of advertising behind it. That does not mean that money alone can make a sustained success out of a poor product or one that has no public acceptance. Max Factor came up with Just Call Me Maxi a few years after the debut of Charlie, spending over $3 million on television advertising alone. With an expenditure of this magnitude, and in an effort to recoup part of the investment quickly, Factor chose to market only toilet waters and colognes, rather than perfume, which is the smallest sales component in a general line. That was to come out at a later date. The company's sales force sold a record amount of a new line to its accounts, and probably overloaded them, for the goods didn't move out of the stores as fast as they came in. The high cost of advertising to introduce a new perfume is so great that only the "biggies" can afford to get in the game.

Gone are the days when Prince Matchabelli, an impoverished Georgian nobleman, could parlay a title and a family formula into a profitable perfume business in the course of a few years. Matchabelli was so strapped financially, he could go out only at night, in a dinner jacket, for all of his other clothes were in hock. He either brought with him from Russia his grandmother's perfume formula or he found one, and, with the very little money he could borrow and with absolutely no qualifications for the perfume business, he prepared to launch his fragrance. A friend in the publicity business arranged an interview with *Collier's* magazine, but forewarned the prince that he must be prepared to tell the writer something that would impress her with his knowledge about perfumes. The reporter went through the preliminary questions about his background and then asked, "Did you always have such a good olfactory sense?"

"I'll tell you how good," the prince replied. "When I was a student in Torino, I used to go to the opera every night, for I adored opera. I became infatuated with one of the prima donnas and I sent her a bouquet every time she sang, with a note declaring my love and inviting her to dine with me in a *salon privé* at a restaurant. She had always refused, but one night she sent a reply that she would take me to her flat. Everything went fine, she was as passionate as I had imagined and we made beautiful love. In the middle of the night, I had to leave; I had endured her perfume as long as I could. She used violet instead of jasmine. That's how good my olfactory senses are!"

Everyone is not endowed with an olfactory sense equal to that of the prince, but despite the persuasions of the advertisement, a woman should wear what she likes, unless the man in her life disagrees with her choice. Some women ignore fashion changes in fragrances and continue to wear one they've used for years; others keep a collection and alternate according to their moods. With the small-size flacons now available, an assortment does not represent too serious an investment. If a perfume is too expensive, then I'd advise buying the same fragrance in the toilet water, which is a less concentrated version and has a more limited staying power.

One of the first lessons we have to teach young copywriters is never to refer to a perfume as a "scent" or an "odor," nor to promise the reader that if she buys certain perfumes she will be chased around by mad violinists or that she will transform meek men into savage beasts. That's too great a responsibility to assume. Why hasn't one of the great perfumers come up with an ad that reads, "Our perfume smells better"? That's what it's all about.

Unlike most other personal articles people buy, jewelry is not bought for adornment but for sentimental or economic reasons, or a combination of both. It is purchased either to celebrate or commemorate some important occasion, or as an investment which can be converted to cash if necessary or transported easily across national borders. Even the romanticist likes to feel that he's making a good buy, but unless he has studied jewelry as assiduously as the dealer, he'll never know how good his buy was until he tries to dispose of it. Comparative shopping is fine and is recommended as a way of acquiring general knowledge about the color, size, and value, but, in the final analysis, the decision is going to have to be made on the basis of which dealer the buyer chooses to believe. Few customers, except for the semipros, can look at a diamond through a high-powered microscope and see what's in the stone. Usually, they end up seeing what the seller tells them is there. Anyone with normal eyesight can tell the difference between a diamond with a yellow cast and one that is blue-white, but not one in a thousand can differentiate between the several gradations of blue-white.

The process of buying a precious stone is not unlike walking through a minefield. There are countless traps and explosive charges to avoid; these require the guidance of an expert with a marked map. There are many reputable jewelers who provide such help and will stand behind their representations. A few of them operate on a single-price policy; they will accept no offers on their merchandise, since they have priced it fairly in the first place. If I were buying a stone, with the knowledge I have of the jewelry business, I would choose such a dealer in preference to one whose prices are subject to bargaining. I would never buy from a "pocket" dealer who travels around the country with his stock in his pocket, for I would never be sure that I could locate him if something went wrong and I could never be positive his merchandise wasn't "hot." I would never buy a jewel at auction because there is limited responsibility after the sale and because there is always the chance that the sale has been rigged by collusive gem dealers. I would select a jeweler with a reputation for fair dealing, whose design taste I liked, and who would treat me as a client to whom he expected to make other sales in the future and not as a one-shot customer.

This advice pertains to the purchase of stones, but it also applies in principle to decorative pieces of jewelry, like bracelets and necklaces, where the mountings represent a significant part of the price. If a piece is ever sold or broken up, the buyer will find there is very little value in the mounting; the money recovered will be for the wholesale cost of the stones plus the melt-up worth of the metal. If fine stones were used, there will be a better price than if second-quality material was used.

This is an important factor for the buyer to consider, for there are two basic types of jewelers and jewelry. There are jewelers who make classic styles with fine material, and there are those who make gold "costume" jewelry, using large stones of inferior quality but with great flair and flash. This latter kind can be very chic and give great pleasure, but has very little value in a break-up.

There are always those who think they can beat the game by picking up an emerald in Colombia, a sapphire or star ruby in India, or a diamond in Antwerp. They usually end up with an inferior stone—sometimes a fake—at more than they would have paid had they purchased it from a good jeweler at home; a bargain is a rarity. Many who have bought gems in India find on return that the stones were backed with colored foil to intensify the shade or that they had been sold a "doublet," a stone in which a thin slice of the colored stone has been cemented to a larger base of valueless zircon. There is little likelihood that the shop will make restitution or even answer a cable.

So-called wholesale prices for stones should be regarded with a certain amount of skepticism, mixed with common sense. A buyer tempted by such offerings, sometimes advertised in respectable publications, should ask himself the question, "Why should this company, in Antwerp or New York, want to take the extra time and effort to sell me a single stone at a period in time when they could make a much larger sale to a wholesale purchaser, or aren't his goods fine enough to sell to the professionals?" The answer is: "It doesn't make sense."

Next to the bargain hunter in the ranking of the dupes come the "story buyers," who are suckers for any piece of jewelry to which there is a story attached, particularly if there is a famous name involved. Leading the list of such names are Marie Antoinette and Carlota of Mexico, both of whom have been dead so long that it is futile to track down the authenticity of the attribution. There have been more Carlota rings sold in New Orleans than she could have worn in a lifetime, even if she changed them every hour in the day. Paris is the center for the Marie Antoinette trade, as well it should be. There, a persevering buyer can pick up a dozen necklaces in a few hours, with the verbal, not written, assurances they belonged to the queen. Some dealers, recognizing this credulity, concoct sustaining stories worthy of soap-opera writers. Moral: buy stones, not stories.

In the trade, the word "gemstone" is used to describe a jewel of superb and ultimate quality. There aren't too many stones which can be given this label honestly, and if and when available, they fetch very high prices, far above those of average quality. Some collect gemstones, others wear them, and still others deal in them, so there is always a market for them. In grades below this classification, there is a vastly larger amount of mineral material which, when cut, properly satisfies the needs and wants of 95 percent of the buying public. With the variety of stones having differing structural formations and subtle color gradations, it is exceedingly difficult to evolve exact definitions that accurately describe the state of perfection and color, in colored stones particularly. What is red in a ruby? Two people may have different ideas. "Pigeon blood" is a name given to describe a certain color of red, but if this is so, then there are some pigeons badly in need of Geritol.

Since diamonds are more consistent in structure than colored stones, it is possible to cut them to a higher standard of perfection. A person buying a diamond in the past twenty years has been able to get a stone infinitely better cut than at any time in history. Of all the jewels, diamonds have the most universal appeal and the easiest convertibility into cash. That is why Europeans living in unstable political climates have long been purchasers of five-carat round diamonds for investment purposes. If they were forced to leave the country hurriedly, they could take a fortune in stones in a money belt far more easily than the equivalent value in paintings or gold. Diamonds are an investor's best friend; they are portable.

———————

When a group of cigar aficionados gathers, it is not unusual to hear one of them remark, "Cuban cigars just aren't as good as they were before Castro." As a fairly recent convert to cigars, I can't judge the validity of that statement, particularly when the only proof offered is the memory of some old-timers. I've smoked cigars made in Cuba, Jamaica, the Canary Islands, Brazil, Mexico, Honduras, Nicaragua, and south Florida, and, to my taste, the Cuban cigar is better today than any other cigar, both in tobacco and make. Since Cuban cigars can't be obtained legally in the United States, I smoke the Jamaican-made Partagas, which suit me better than the others, but when I go to Europe, I luxuriate with a genuine Havana.

Growing tobacco for cigars has some similarities to growing grapes for wine. It has been rumored that Cuban tobacco seed was smuggled to a number of countries in the Caribbean where agricultural experts suggested there were soil and climatic conditions similar to those of Cuba. If the stories are true, then the results have been unsuccessful, for none of these trials have resulted in the production of a close imitation of the Cuban product, any more than the transplanting of the vines of Burgundy grapes will assure the growth of a Romanée Conti or a Richebourg in California or Chile. You can get good wine from those areas, but you can't reproduce the original. Sun, rainfall, drainage, temperature, all have an effect on the final product, with the result that there are good and poor years for wines, and for the same reasons there are good and poor years for tobacco.

So far, Cuba's shortage in trading currency has prevented

*Search for
the Best:
Taste and
Smell*

———

123

the importation of chemical fertilizers and any sizable amount of cigar-making machinery. Tobacco is grown, fertilized, stored, and aged in the same manner as in the days before Castro. Machines are used for making cigars of the cheaper grades of tobacco, which are exported mainly to the Communist-country markets. Fortunately for cigar smokers, the lack of money for machinery has forced Cuban factories to continue to make their best cigars by hand. When I made my first trip to Russia and Poland, I didn't take any cigars with me, for I felt confident I would find ample supplies of fine Cuban cigars in the Communist countries. The Havanas available had the familiar labels, but they were obviously not prime quality. The cigars were scarred, rough, and uneven in color, and it was only later that my friend Davidoff, the great tobacco merchant in Geneva and one of the world's largest buyers of Cuban cigars, explained that Cuba reserved its prime-quality cigars for the hard-currency countries, trading its lesser grades to those nations which operate on the barter system.

For reasons of sentiment and tradition, Spain is given a buying preference over other countries but, since the distribution of tobacco is a state monopoly run by civil servants, Spain does not necessarily get the best cigars. England and Switzerland are the two most important markets for fine cigars, and that is where the cigar buyer will find the best selections and the finest quality. Dunhill in London and Davidoff in Geneva and Zurich are the largest fine-cigar retailers in their respective countries. The properties of the cigar manufacturers were expropriated at the time of the revolution, but the Cuban government maintained the operation of the various factories, each producing its traditional blends and brands. The original owners fled to other countries, and many set up cigar factories in the Canary Islands, Jamaica, and Florida.

With the possibility of normal relations being re-established between Cuba and the United States, cigar smokers have been looking forward to being able to buy Montecristo, Punch, and Partagas cigars in the United States. If, and when, that time comes, there will be disputes, however, as to who owns the trademarks in the United States, for the Partagas brand now being made in Jamaica is sold under that name already, and Montecristo, Upmann, and others are produced in the Canary Islands. It may become necessary to market the famous Cuban brands in the United States under different names, such as Davidoff's Château Margaux and Dunhill's Don Alfredo, to avoid costly and lengthy lawsuits, for it is unlikely that the Cuban government will decide to pay restitution to the expropriated owners. All of that will be unimportant to the smokers who will be glad to have the opportunity to smoke Cuban cigars legally under any name.

Brand preference is greatly a matter of individual taste and it is difficult to get even the professionals to agree on a rating. One leading London tobacco merchant was willing to give me his own personal grading, but not for attribution:

1. Montecristo
2. Romeo y Julieta
3. H. Upmann
4. Bolivar
5. Ramon Allones
6. Partagas
7. Por Larrañaga
8. Punch
9. Hoyo de Monterrey
10. Rey del Mundo

A cigar authority from another country gave me his confidential rating in a slightly different format, but also on the basis of anonymity:

Quality	*Strength*
1. Montecristo	1. Punch
2. Punch	2. Montecristo
3. H. Upmann	3. H. Upmann
4. Romeo y Julieta	4. Partagas
5. Partagas	5. Ramon Allones
6. Por Larrañaga	6. Por Larrañaga
7. Ramon Allones	7. Romeo y Julieta

The variations in grading between these lists of two qualified and experienced dealers are indicative of the fact that there

Search for the Best: Taste and Smell

is wide room for disagreements among experts in matters of taste and smell. It is impossible to declare that one is right and the other wrong. They are both right.

Demand for Cuban cigars is greater than ever; supply is restricted by the capacity of the choicest land to produce more leaf, and prices are continuing to increase.

The price of a top-quality Cuban cigar will vary from $2 to $4, depending on brand and size, which has caused many smokers to switch to pipes as a matter of economy. The initial cost of a new pipe can vary from $25 to $100, but the tobacco cost is low and matches are free. With some exceptions, pipes are made from the roots of the brier, a shrub of the heath genus, the best of which come from Algeria. The quality of the pipe is dependent on the choice of the brier root, its seasoning, and the degree of handwork in the cutting, shaping, and polishing processes. There is a world shortage of good brier; only one-half of one percent of the briers are good enough for top-quality pipes. There are a dozen or more classic forms made by almost all factories and, in addition, there are the free-form pipes, originated in Denmark, fashioned by carvers who have a greater sense of poetry than good design.

Some pipes are made with a smooth, polished surface, and some are sandblasted for a rough texture. In this process, the bowl of the pipe is sandblasted to erode the softer parts of the brier, leaving the tougher grain in relief. The discovery of sandblasting was an accident, resulting from a pipe having been left near a boiler, the heat from which burned out the soft areas. It was a logical step then to use sandblasting as a technique to accomplish the same result. This process is valuable to all pipemakers, for after a pipe has been rough-carved, certain blemishes, or small pits, in the brier show up. These holes can be filled to achieve uniformity of finish, but such a pipe cannot be marketed as top quality. Sandblasting does away with these superficial imperfections, and such pipes can then be sold as perfect. Only good-quality briers can be put through this process, for low grades would be completely eroded under the pressure. Actually, there are advantages to a sandblasted pipe from the smoker's point of view. The surface of the bowl, being almost doubled, permits heat to radiate faster, thus cooling the pipe. It is lighter in weight (which the teeth appreciate) and, having a rough surface, it never looks dull or scratched. Finally, it is 20 percent less expensive than the same model unblasted.

The manner in which the grain of the wood is cut can be a factor in the price of the pipe, without contributing to its smoking qualities. There is more waste in the cutting of the root, so that the grain is straight, but such a pipe has no particular virtue other than appearance. A cut emphasizing the burl pattern of the wood is also attractive and less expensive than a straight grain. The best pipe store I've ever come across is Iwan Ries on Wabash Avenue in Chicago. Not only does it have the largest selection of pipes from all makers and in all qualities but it has the most knowledgeable sales staff I've ever met. In an era when the quality of sales service has deteriorated as much as merchandise, it's a refreshing experience to be waited on by a salesperson who knows what he is talking about and conscientiously tries to give good advice. The store is still family-operated.

Pipes are made all over the world, and each maker proudly contends that his are the best, but, as in cigars, the smokers have their own evaluation system. In England, the top makers are Dunhill, Comoy, and Charatan; in Denmark, they are Ivarsson, Stanwell, and Nording; in Italy, it is Savinelli; in Ireland, it is Peterson. The best meerschaums are produced by Pioneer Pipe of Brooklyn.

Habit de Musicien.

A Paris, Chez N. de L'Armessin, Rue S.t Jacques, à la Pome d'Or.   Avec Privil. du Roy.

8

The Seduction of the Buyer

The quality and price of what we, as customers, buy may be affected by many factors, including payola given to the retail or wholesale buyers. A prominent businessman with an overview into dozens of industries made the assertion: "Fifty to seventy-five percent of all merchandise and goods purchased by professional buyers is based on considerations other than the merit of the product."

At the time an employee was appointed to a buyer's position, I made it a practice to call the person to my office and deliver "the new buyer's lecture," which went something like this: "In your new position you have many responsibilities but only one obligation. That obligation is to purchase the best merchandise that our money can buy from the most reliable resources in the markets. By 'best' we mean best in workmanship, in fabric, in fashion, at a fair price that enables the manufacturer to make a profit and stay in business. After one year, during which you will familiarize yourself with our resource structure, you will be free to choose your own suppliers, with the approval of your merchandise supervisor, but until you have learned your job, you do not have the privilege of dropping a manufacturer unless you can prove conclusively that he is either dishonest or dishonorable.

"As a buyer your greatest strength will be your freedom to buy on the basis of merit, but you will find that many contending sellers will try to influence your judgment and orders in a variety of ways. Some may curry your favor by entertainment at dinner, theater, sporting events; others by expensive gifts at Christmas and birthdays; others may offer outright bribes in the form of a kickback of two to five percent of your purchases. We frown on the acceptance of costly gifts and would urge you to return them or to make a return gift of comparable monetary value. If we should ever find that you have accepted payola in the form of a commission, you will be immediately terminated and we shall prosecute you to the fullest extent of the law.

"Any commitment you make in writing signed by your merchandise manager this company will honor, but we will not tolerate the 'kiting' of orders [verbal assurances that merchandise orders will be confirmed in writing at a subsequent date]. That is also a cause for instant dismissal.

"The ways of seduction are many: beware!"

We never caught anyone taking a bribe, but we did fire several who couldn't resist the temptation to kite orders. Possibly the most insidious form of corruption is simple friendship that develops between buyer and seller; the kind of relationship that subconsciously influences a buyer to give a preference to a friend. We couldn't tell buyers not to be friendly, for that's an unnatural restriction, besides which, a friendly manufacturer can be legitimately helpful in a variety of ways, such as early deliveries, return privileges, and advice.

Buyers get lonely on a buying trip and their expense allowances barely cover their basic costs, so when a salesman offers to take them out on the town, it's very tempting. The next day it is difficult to look at the salesman's line with complete objectivity. A weekend invitation to a manufacturer's summer home in the Hamptons establishes a warmth of relationship that can lead the buyer to feel a desire to reciprocate by increasing the size of the order. A pair of tickets to the Super Bowl and air transportation can make a purchasing agent feel a moral obligation to choose his benefactor's product over competition, even though there's a slight difference in price between the two. Sometimes it's the boss who has been seduced, and he passes down the word as to who gets the business.

I recall one incident of seduction on my first market trip as a buyer, when Al Neiman, my uncle and director of the buying activities of the store, said, "Last night I was at a party with Louie Brenner and he's opening his new line tomorrow. I want to go in and write the largest order he'll get. We'll give him an order for fifty thousand dollars." This was before he had even had a chance to see and evaluate the merit of the line. It was a decision made on the basis of his friendship for Mr. Brenner and his desire to be a big-shot buyer.

Over the long haul, this kind of favoritism probably doesn't affect the value of the product to the consumer too much. The monetary payoff is the most vicious form of payola, for the buyer on the take purchases an inferior product in some quantity to make it worthwhile for himself. This is a practice that is particularly prevalent in the fur industry. I asked the head of a personnel-placement firm if he could name more than three fur buyers in the United States who were not on the take either at the present or at some time in the past; his reply was, "I know of only two I'd swear are clean." Instead of buying the best, the "takers" buy the goods that pay *them* the best, and the customer ends up with an inferior fur garment.

Many manufacturers give payola in the form of free articles of apparel or, at least, very large discounts, to buyers and members of the fashion staff. Most retailers have been reluctant to move in against this source of gravy. The manufacturer justifies it, with some reason, on the grounds that as buyers wear his articles on the selling floors, salespeople as well as customers become impressed and that he derives beneficial advertising at the point of sale. On one occasion, we had a manufacturer who wanted to extend this discount privilege to all salespeople in the department handling his line, which we rejected for the reason that such a practice would be discriminatory against other lines not offering comparable discounts and that customers might very well be prevented from seeing our full assortments.

Free or discounted apparel is a common courtesy shown to the editors of the fashion publications. Since most manufacturers participate, it's difficult to see where anyone gains, but since all do it, a nonpractitioner would be placed at a great competitive disadvantage. In nonvenal journalism, the reporter is free to report on the basis of news value of the story. In fashion journalism, the most newsworthy items may be sublimated to the pressure of the manufacturer who may have his own private reasons for pushing one article over another, with the net result that the magazine's reader may or may not be shown that which is the best in the market. It is axiomatic that if a retailer is a nonadvertiser in the fashion journals, it is unlikely that his name will ever be given the coveted credit lines, and that if a textile mill and an airline purchase blocks of advertisements, they will receive reciprocal editorial pages featuring their products or services.

Buyers can become intimidated by a famous designer or captivated by a handsome salesperson and be influenced just as surely as by money. I recall one instance of that nature quite a few years ago when I was going through the gift shop with the buyer to see some recent imports from Italy. I was complimenting him on his selections until my eye spied a large, overdecorated piece of ceramic in garish colors. I was shocked that a buyer with superb taste could have been guilty of buying such a monstrosity. Pointing to it, I suggested, "This must be something the manufacturer shipped you in error, for I'm sure you never could have bought it."

To his credit, he refused to take the easy way out I had given him. "No," he replied, "it was purchased during a momentary lapse of judgment."

For a moment I thought he was going to tell me that he had succumbed to payola. "How and why? Tell me the whole truth," I insisted.

"Well, at this factory's showroom, there was a gorgeous blonde who had the biggest pair of boobs I've ever seen. When she came to this piece on the shelf and recommended it as their latest masterpiece, I was so entranced by her that I said 'Yes' when I meant to say 'No.' "

This was the most honest admission of a mistake by a buyer I had ever heard, so I said, "Since you're no longer under her spell, smash the piece, take a markdown on it, and tell your merchandise man that I accidentally knocked it off the counter."

Store managements, themselves, are equally guilty in

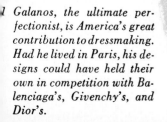

Galanos, the ultimate perfectionist, is America's great contribution to dressmaking. Had he lived in Paris, his designs could have held their own in competition with Balenciaga's, Givenchy's, and Dior's.

Sketch: *Neiman-Marcus*

2 A Neiman-Marcus fashion
exclusive by America's premier
designer, James Galanos, in
rare, natural cross fox pelts.

3

3 The hands of a skilled tailor
make the hundreds of tiny
stitches that insure softness
of construction and the permanent shaping of the garment. Shown here is a detail
of an Oxxford jacket in the
course of being made.

4 *Eli Zabar left his family's large and successful delicatessen business to open his own small gourmet shop, E.A.T., on upper Madison Avenue. There he caters to the gourmets instead of the big eaters.*

5 *Beluga caviar is the largest egg produced by the Beluga sturgeon; when properly packed, it is the premium caviar on the world market. It is imported by Iron Gate Products Co. of New York.*

6 *Château Petrus, produced on an eighteen-acre estate in the commune of Pomerol, has more body and vigor than most of the wines of Bordeaux. It was first popularized in the United States by the late Henri Soulé.*

7 *The Sprüngli confectionary store and tea shop in Zurich makes a wafer-thin carré with cream centers of raspberry, strawberry, orange, and lemon covered by a coating of dark chocolate. Sprüngli carrés have no equal.*

8 *Caffè Greco, on the Via Condotti in Rome, is the favorite espresso bar of thousands of coffee lovers, who savor the aroma as well as the flavor of its brew, made from a particular blend of charred beans.*

7

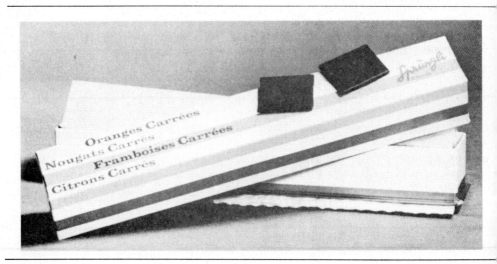

Photograph: Ralph Crane, *Life* Magazine © 1949, 1977 Time Inc.

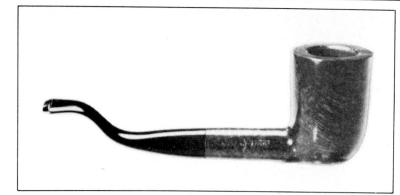

9 The "Chairman's Pipe" by Savinelli has a reverse curved stem that discourages moisture from draining back into the mouth and that lowers the pipe an additional half inch from the line of vision.

10 The "Perfection" pattern of crystal wine goblets by Baccarat is the paradigm of all wine glasses. Paperthin, a goblet will bend under the pressure of forefinger and thumb.

10

Courtesy Baccarat Crystal

11 Steuben spares no effort in producing the most beautiful glass in the world. "Cityscapes" by Lloyd Atkins was commissioned, as are works executed by other leading contemporary artists.

12 *Throughout the world, the most popular Havana cigar is the Montecristo. It is still handmade in the same factory as in pre-Castro days and maintains the same standards of quality and blending.*

14 *One of the few things that is as good as it used to be is* The New Yorker *magazine, which has weathered changes in editorial direction without changes in quality and format.*

13

13 *Peugeot pepper mills are made by the producer of France's sturdiest automobile. The mechanism of the pepper mill is cast from high-quality tempered steel and is expected to last forever.*

15 Sara Lee pound cake is noble enough to grace a Royal Crown Derby cake plate and moderate enough in price to go into a lunch pail. It has survived changes in ownership and the popularization brought on by mass production.

17 The London taxi and driver are unique. The cab is roomy, comfortable, and clean; the driver is invariably polite and knowledgeable, and takes seriously his responsibility to operate a "publicly licensed vehicle."

16

16 The most luxurious table cutlery in the world is made by Peter of the Faubourg St. Honoré in Paris. This pattern, called "Octogone," has handles of a semiprecious mineral.

Photograph: James R. Robinson, Inc.

Photograph: The British Tourist Authority

Habit de Chapellier

Habit de Tailleur

Habit de Barbier Perruquier

Habit de Cordonnier

Habit de Musicien

Habit de Fourreur

18 *A Tradesmen's Scarf printed on a pure silk thirty-six-
inch square, reproducing
six of the Larmessin* Costumes Grotesques, *from
the Neiman-Marcus library
of fashion.*

taking payola. They get it in the form of cooperative advertising money from the manufacturers whose names are carried in the headlines or in the body of the copy. In itself there's nothing wrong with this practice, for it seems only fair that the manufacturer share in the cost of publicizing his merchandise and corporate identity. Most manufacturers set a definite sum aside for promotional purposes, related to the retailer's annual purchases. As one of the inventors of this device, some forty years ago, I have come to rue the day of my ingenuity, for "co-op money," as it's called, has become a pernicious influence in retail advertising, often depriving the customer from seeing the best and the most newsworthy merchandise in advertisements. With constantly rising newspaper-space costs, store advertising managers throw out the best merchandise story if it has no subsidy in favor of a poorer one that has money behind it. Very quickly, the buyers learn not to bring up superior merchandise for advertising, because in many cases that character and quality of product comes either from smaller makers who can't afford to provide advertising allowances or from name designers who demand a free ride. This, then, becomes an explanation as to why retail advertising has deteriorated so markedly in the quality of its merchandise content. The situation might be accurately compared to a newspaper which restricted its news stories to those individuals and countries that paid a fixed space rate.

Cosmetics demonstrations originated when they were first used as traveling emissaries to introduce new products to the public over the toiletry-department counters. These factory-trained salespeople proved so successful that the bright minds of the aggressive cosmetic industry figured out the idea of having permanent specially trained representatives who would sell their products exclusively. An arrangement was made whereby a salesperson would be assigned to a specific line and would become the employee of the cosmetic firm she represented rather than of the store. The store was relieved of the salary costs and the responsibility of training. In addition, the manufacturers made deals for specific space locations within the departments, paying an agreed sum for the showcases, either in cash or free merchandise. This payola is not under the counter (no pun intended), but, straightforward as it is, it is still a payoff.

Such manufacturer "reps" are experts in their own lines, but know nothing about other lines in the department, nor will they make any effort to serve the customer who may request another product. "Go over to the counter across the aisle" would be their maximum bit of assistance. All of this makes a very profitable deal for the retailer, but a bad one, in my opinion, for the customer, who comes into the store to shop with the store and not with an individual maker.

Adam Gimbel disliked this scheme for that very reason and devised what has come to be known as the "Saks plan," which said to the cosmetic industry: "No salespersons at Saks can be employees of a manufacturer; they are all employees of Saks and must serve any customer who comes into the department for whatever the customer wants. Pay us the commission you are paying directly to your representatives and we will pass it on, in toto, to the person assigned to your line. Furthermore, we will undertake to perform training in your line as well as all others we sell. When your sales managers come to our stores, they can give specialized training to our entire staff." The industry didn't like it, but Saks was too big to fight and they yielded, begrudgingly. To my knowledge, Neiman-Marcus is the only other major retailer that has adopted the Saks plan and has stayed with it over the years.

But buyers and stores aren't the only victims of payola. Customers have always been subject to the seduction of misleading advertising and spurious claims, but within the last decade they have fallen victim to one of the most successful merchandising devices in mercantile history—the cosmetic gift-with-purchase. Dramatic full-color mailing pieces and television commercials offer the customers free gifts with values varying from $25.00 to $50.00 with the purchase of $8.95 of the X cosmetics line. Whether the free-gift valuation is bona fide or not is immaterial, but this new promotional technique diverts the customer's attention from what may be best to what is free.

Its proponents will contend that it is the most effective way to introduce a new, fine-quality product. Its detractors will claim that the quality of the product is put in secondary position to the size and attractiveness of the free offer. Cosmetics manufacturers or retailers cannot ignore this new selling tool, even if they disagree with its philosophy. It's simply impossible to build volume and retain a competitive market position without participating in the free-gift race. The cost of a full-scale, gift-with-purchase program is so great that it is very difficult or nearly impossible for a new maker with a medium-size investment to get into the cosmetics business today, even with a superior product.

So, the availability of the best in cosmetics today is affected by the best the large companies produce and not by the infusion of new products from small makers operating in a genuinely competitive economy.

In the drive for profitability, many retailers and their buyers have shifted their business from manufacturers who make the best goods to those who will provide additional inducements, which are costly and must eventually reflect themselves in the price of the product or in a reduction in quality of the merchandise. This was commented on by Sanford Josephson in a column, "The Big Hitters Are Getting Sluggish," which appeared in the *Daily News Record:* "Department stores should spend less time worrying about what merchandise they can return and how much markdown money they're going to get . . . and more time worrying about how they can sell merchandise once it's in the store."

Buyers pride themselves on being able to work out deals with manufacturers, but they seem to be unaware that nothing in life comes free and that they eventually pay for continuous privileges. I am a strong proponent of hard trading in the first place, but believe that after the deal is made both parties should stand by their bargain.

The garment manufacturer is not the only one who shapes the merchandise selections that get into retail advertising, for the largest spenders, by far, are the giant yarn spinners and weavers, who discovered they could influence both the cutters and retailers by offering subsidy money for the use and advertising of their products. There is no subterfuge involved, for their identification is clearly indicated, but the fact that the retailer can get advertising money if he stipulates the use of certain yarns or cloths leads him to switch from non-revenue-producing fabrics. This has proved to be a most successful way to get a new fabric into general consumption.

Du Pont employed this technique to popularize its Qiana® fiber, Hoechst Mills spent hundreds of thousands of dollars to promote its Trevira® yarn, and even the suppliers of interlining (when they were in use) spent money to get retailers to request the use of specific brands of interlinings. The customer never saw the interlining and couldn't have cared less, but, because a large producer was underwriting retail advertising on garments interlined with his material, Si Bonne®, buyers insisted that their manufacturers switch brands of interlining. The Wool Bureau, a cooperative organization financed by levies on wool growers to combat the competition of the synthetic industry, even requires the inclusion of its trademark in every ad to qualify for reimbursement. These "bugs," as they are called in the trade, add nothing to the graphic beauty of the advertising but do enrich the coffers of the stores' advertising budgets.

Obviously, the big producers lead in the disbursement of this type of payola, just as they would be the largest spenders in national advertising space if they weren't able to get into the retailers' ads. The big would out-advertise the small, and, depending on the effectiveness of their campaigns and the merits of their products, they would eventually succeed or fail in creating a consumer demand; but, at least, they would not be in the position of buying their way into retailer specifications and stocks. The current method restricts the customer's freedom of choice, it encourages greater standardization, and it makes it less likely that the best can get a chance to reach the marketplace.

The disadvantageous effect of co-op advertising goes even further. It leads to vendor labels and hang-tags which, in the guise of providing cleaning instructions, also carry an advertisement from the manufacturer—who in effect is saying, "Take my money, take my tags." Some garments carry multiple labels and tags, not only of the maker but of the yarn company and the weaver as well. The only thing lacking so far is a manufacturer's label showing a picture of his son at his bar mitzvah. The tags become intertwined, making it more difficult to extricate a garment from the racks; they interfere with the ease of trying on merchandise; and they are unsightly.

This dependence on vendor money prevents the stores from doing imaginative, image-building advertisements that establish and reiterate the identification of the store itself, from creating motivational advertising that contributes to the enhancement of the store's mystique as a leader in its particular aspect of distribution.

Equally notorious as the fur industry for the prevalence of payola is the food business at the restaurant and hotel levels. An unhappy executive chef can find plenty of reasons to reject deliveries of fish, fowl, and meat, so it's easier to pay him off than to have to accept returns of spoiled food. To compensate for his extra cost, the supplier either buries the commission he pays in his invoice or he takes it out of the quality. Since there are so many variables in raw-food products, it becomes very difficult to detect minor depreciations in quality. Perhaps that's the reason you get a tough steak or a tasteless chicken.

The most sophisticated hotel operations now require three bids on all purchases, and with the use of computers, violations of policy are more easily detected, but not eliminated. All directors of first-class hotels will swear they buy the finest food on the market, but that doesn't mean that they get them. Some food and beverage managers and chefs have retired as very rich men.

Most stores and manufacturers use buying offices or agents, particularly abroad, to scout the markets and handle the payment and shipment of purchases, for which they pay a buying commission of 5 to 10 percent of the amount of goods delivered. Some agents and some employees of the offices also collect a rake-off from the factories. This is known as "taking it both ways." The maker may squeeze this cost out of the

The Seduction of the Buyer

quality of the product, or he may add it into his calculations as a cost of doing business. Assuredly, this practice does not add to the quality of the merchandise.

About twenty states have statutes which make commercial bribery a first-degree misdemeanor, thus enabling companies to prosecute buyers for accepting kickbacks. Several years ago, W. T. Grant charged that several members of their real-estate department had been bribed in an attempt to "restrict competition by limiting Grant's access to other shopping-center developers and landlords." J. C. Penney, Inc., sued a former employee and several contractors for $23 million "over an alleged bribery scheme said to have inflated the value of work and material used during construction at Penney's New York headquarters," according to *Women's Wear Daily*. J. M. Fields, a discount–department-store chain, won a judgment of $212,762 against a former member of its staff, "in a case which backed the right of an employer to recover the salary paid to an employee taking kickbacks. The employee, now living in Hong Kong, is appealing the judgment," said *WWD*.

In an interesting survey headlined, "The Ancient Art of the Kickback," *WWD* speculates that the practice nets dishonest executives $10 billion to $15 billion a year. *WWD* quotes a former coat manufacturer as saying: "It's impossible for anybody to survive in this business without paying off. There are people on top of you, below you, to the side of you—it's ultracompetitive. The only question the manufacturer asks himself is not whether he should pay, but rather, 'Am I giving the buyer enough?'"

Some manufacturers explain that they keep their showrooms open on Saturday as a way of making cash sales to retail customers to provide them with unreported income which can be used to pay off the store buyers who are too smart to accept checks. The IRS is interested in this aspect of the matter, and the postal authorities and FBI can move in on any use of the mails in dummy invoicing schemes or interstate telephone calls made to work out the details of the payola.

But *Women's Wear Daily* ends its article with a cynical conclusion, the cynicism of *déjà vu:* "Clearly, kickback schemes range across all facets of retailing and manufacturing and involve many people. The practice seems unstoppable, at least at the buyer level where nearly 400 offices clog New York alone."

It can be argued that the payola situation has come about as the result of low salaries paid to store buyers and market representatives. This might have been true a dozen years ago, but salaries in the buying field have advanced sharply. I believe that if a buyer has larceny in his heart, he will simply boost his income, whatever his salary might be. Others will contend that the kickback is one of the unfortunate end products of the competitive system in the struggle for survival. Who is there to say that a fur buyer taking his $10,000 bribe is any worse than the politician accepting $200,000 to influence legislation, or a Lockheed or Northrop, to sell their planes, paying off millions to foreign purchasers? At some time, society will have to answer this question.

Now, I'm not so naïve as to suggest that business is any more corrupt than it ever was. It might even be less so. I am well aware of the fact that the twin movements of consumerism and reform have put the spotlight of publicity on business wrongdoing, and have conditioned the public to expect a higher standard of ethics from business at all levels.

I also recognize that communications have improved so vastly that a crime committed in Duluth becomes known in Dallas the night it is discovered. Fifty years ago, it might have taken people in Dallas six months to learn about it. So I don't think business is worse. It's just that our flaws show up much faster today than they used to.

Businessmen who have been involved in these practices argue that they are traditional business customs locally and are necessary to compete with foreign business firms; necessary for Northrop to sell airplanes in the Middle East . . . for Exxon to do business in Italy . . . for United Brands to do business in Honduras . . . for Gulf Oil to do business in Bolivia . . . for Lockheed to sell planes in Japan. They also argue that many of the payments are perfectly legal, in a technical sense.

The Seduction of the Buyer

Perhaps so, but, in my judgment, those practices pose a great moral dilemma for our nation in general and for the American business community in particular. Our culture is based on the Judeo-Christian code of ethics, which espouses lofty moral standards of fair and honest dealing. Now, however, we seem to have revised those standards. We still talk about dealing honorably and forthrightly with people. But we're saying that we believe in this credo domestically, but it doesn't apply overseas. In other words, to hell with the foreigner; we insist on honest scales at the supermarket but not for overseas shipments of grain.

I don't believe we can get away with that. I don't believe a double standard works—whether you're an individual, a corporation, or a nation. Sooner or later, your right hand becomes affected by what your left hand is doing. How long will it be before we start asking ourselves: "Well, it works overseas; why not try it at home?" Is it already happening? Is it just coincidence that some of the companies which have admitted illegal political contributions overseas have also admitted to the same practice here at home?

So I reject the voices which defend unethical American business practices abroad. I reject the cynical attitude of former Treasury Secretary John Connally, who said that too many U.S. enterprises overseas have had to use "fang and claw" to operate because the U.S. State Department gives them little or no support. When Mr. Connally tries to tell us that it is time to "curb the insidious feeling of guilt" over the problems of the world, we need to ask him what else but guilt and alarm are we supposed to feel as we watch the United States adding to those problems on a daily basis?

America is supposed to stand for something special in this world. We're not supposed to get down in the mud with the other nations; we're supposed to be a beacon for other nations to follow. Our behavior is supposed to be different; that's what the American ideal is all about. Our credo should not be, "When in Rome, do as the Romans do." Rather, it should be, "When in Rome, do as Americans are supposed to do." I think, by and large, we have earned the respect of the people of the world, except when we have violated our own code of ethics.

What is the answer to those who say that payola is sometimes necessary to do business overseas? My answer is that you have to pay for a code of ethics; and it doesn't come cheap. Neiman-Marcus decided against entering a profitable foreign market when it became apparent that it would be subjected to a payoff system as the price of admission.

And, again, I ask the question: Can the free-enterprise system survive such abuses? Do we really still believe in the free-enterprise system when we treat competition as if it were poison? Competition is the fuel that makes free enterprise work. Without it, free enterprise becomes corporate enterprise—and there is no corporation in the world that is wise enough to correct its internal mistakes. Competition has a way of correcting them very quickly and very effectively.

Licensing of products and trademarked names is nothing new, because for years companies have licensed the manufacture of their products in foreign countries. The formulas have been followed so faithfully that it has been difficult to tell the difference between the original and the reproduction. Rigid quality controls were set up in the licensing contracts to which there has been faithful adherence. Companies which could not afford to set up worldwide manufacturing facilities were enabled by this technique to get worldwide distribution and to collect profits from royalties. In the past dozen years, with the promotion of designer names, licensing has invaded the fashion industry. Customers who have been impressed by the reputation of a famous fashion name, or who have had satisfactory experience with the original product, find a wide variety of articles on the market bearing the label with which they are familiar. They are seduced into believing that the merchandise was designed by the famous name. Not so!

In the majority of cases, the designer has made a deal to lend his name, for a royalty, to makers of bed sheets, suspenders, sweaters, neckties, scarves, costume jewelry, shoes, and a host of other products which he doesn't design. Frequently, the licensee develops his own designs which he submits to the famous name for approval, who may okay all of them or reject a few. The retail customer pays a premium

The Seduction of the Buyer

of from 10 to 20 percent more for the article than if it bore only the store's label. There are some designers who rigidly control the designs and quality of their licensees. Christian Dior, the first of the French couture houses to go in for licensing on a large scale, made some early mistakes in the selection of licensees, but very quickly corrected them. Today, Dior licenses forty products in twenty-four countries with a distribution network covering more than eighty countries. Dior has succeeded in maintaining a remarkable degree of uniformity, considering the differences in manufacturing sophistication between countries such as Brazil and Germany, Australia and the United States.

Louis Vuitton, the luggage maker of Paris, made hard-side suitcases for the French market which he sold to Saks Fifth Avenue and a few other retailers in the United States. Saks recognized that the big demand in America was for soft-side, no-frame luggage of a type Vuitton was unprepared to make, so they made a deal to get the exclusive importation rights for his famous brown-and-gold imprinted synthetic material bearing the LV initials, with the privilege of passing it on to a domestic maker to manufacture. They selected the French Company of California, which had specialized in the production of soft luggage. Under this arrangement, Vuitton sells the cloth to Saks at a profit plus a royalty, Saks turns the material over to French, which has U.S. exclusive rights to manufacture or subcontract Vuitton luggage, for which it pays a royalty to Saks, with the right to sell the Vuitton luggage to its other accounts as well as to Saks. This complicated importation method with the double royalties makes a four-suiter Vuitton hanging bag retail for $435 as against $265 for the same bag made in French's top-quality imported fabric.

Not all designers in America or France have the desire, skill, or time to design all of the products they have licensed. After a fashion designer has created four to six collections a year, made the necessary personal appearances to sell the lines, traveled to Italy to see the new fabrics, taken vacations, there isn't much time left to devote to designing a multitude of other items. And if he should have the time, does he possess that much knowledge of diversified products to be able to design them? Of course, he may have developed a design studio with assistants to whom he can delegate these responsibilities, in which case the label he sells might more properly read, "From the design studio of *XYZ*."

American designers, also, are in the licensing business, from *A* to *Z*, including *H* for Halston, and I cannot believe that they either select every tie fabric and color in which the patterns are printed, or that they give more than cursory approval to the ranges submitted to them, if that. A designer may tell his licensed shoemaker that he wants a high, thick-heeled shoe with an ankle strap for his new collection, but that's about the maximum direction he gives to the line of shoes which will be sold under his label. Shoes take a long time to produce, and no shoemaker can stand around waiting for a couturier to draw every shoe pattern he wants in his new line. An intelligent shoemaker, like David Evins, forms a pretty accurate idea of the designer's tastes and creates a line he thinks will tie in well with the general fashion trend toward which the designer is moving.

Diane Von Furstenberg permitted the use of her name on a collection of shoes without royalty simply for the publicity the additional advertising would give her name. On the other hand, Balenciaga was very circumspect about the manner in which his name was used, and voluntarily retired from his couture business and closed it in 1968, saying, "When I consider the needs of the women of today, I have nothing to do."

I have no quarrel with designers who exploit their talents to the fullest extent, but I consider it dishonest for them to sell their labels on merchandise to which they have made little or no contribution, and over which they have exercised no quality control, to retail customers who think they are getting some part of the original. The SEC doesn't permit the sale of securities with such flimflam.

Payola comes in green, pink, and, sometimes, with skirts.

*The Seduction
of the Buyer*

Habit de Verrier. Fayencier.

A Paris Chez N de Larmessin Rue S.t Jacques a la Pome d'Or.   Avec Privil du Roy.

9

The Building and Preservation of a Mystique

You can't touch it; it has no smell; it is weightless; it is invisible, but it manifests its being in very tangible ways. It has a digestive system, so it must be fed occasionally to assure continued growth. It is hard to build, but once it has matured, it has remarkable powers of survival. It can be destroyed by neglect over a prolonged period of time and by a repetitious series of tasteless, inelegant, antisocial, tawdry, and/or dishonest activities directed against it. All of that is by way of describing the nature of a mystique, which is formally defined by Webster as a "complex of quasi-mystical attitudes and feelings surrounding some person, institution, or activity."

One thing is certain: it can't be built overnight, even by the most skilled publicists. The PR people can raise a lot of bally-hoo about a new motion-picture star or an institution, but all they accomplish is to turn on the spotlight; it will take time and repeated demonstrations of ability, performance, integrity, and consistency before the mystique emerges. I doubt seriously if anyone has ever achieved a mystique by setting out *consciously* to build one. The core of mystique is an idea —widely and fondly held by a large number of people—that has been built on "remembrances of things past": acts of kindness and thoughtfulness, deeds of courage and conviction, repeated demonstrations of leadership and reliability, proofs of devotion to the public welfare as well as to profits, all tied together by the qualities of humor, talent, and integrity.

Many who strive for fame get it momentarily, or even permanently, without ever acquiring a mystique. It all has to do with the way the public perceives an individual or institution, its appraisal of the genuineness and worthiness of the effort. Put another way, a mystique is the public's way of showing favorable recognition to the repeater who never lets it down. This, then, is an account of the growth of a reputation and its evolution into a mystique.

Bendel's has a mystique, Bonwit's doesn't; Judy Garland had one, as does her daughter Liza Minnelli, Barbra Streisand doesn't; Saint Laurent has it, Cardin doesn't. Abercrombie & Fitch had it, but lost it; Gloria Vanderbilt has always had it, Charlotte Ford never had it; *The New Yorker* earned it, *New York* hasn't; Sophia Loren has held on to it, Gina Lollobrigida never attained one; John Kennedy built one, his successors never knew how; Jackie O had one, but blew it; the Yankees have had one and have kept it; Neiman-Marcus has one, its imitators do not.

The word "mystique" is always used with a favorable connotation; at least, I've never heard of anyone having a bad mystique. Mystique is another way of saying, "reputation," which Emma Carleton defined as "a bubble which man bursts when he tries to blow it for himself." I had no idea I was helping to build a mystique when I entered Neiman-Marcus to start my business career. It was a small, family business with a good local reputation for integrity, fashion leadership, and quality, and I proceeded to build on those solid assets to attain national recognition. I wanted our customers to be tremendously proud of the Neiman-Marcus label in their fur coats, and I reasoned that if their friends in other states knew something about the store, the N-M customers would bask in reflected glory. I coined the sentence, "Neiman-Marcus sells more high-quality merchandise than any store between New York and California," and a phrase, "More fine merchandise under one roof than any store in the country." I used them in speeches and in out-of-town press interviews until I had the satisfaction of hearing customers, unconscious of the fact that

I had been the original source, play them back to me.

I owe much of what I learned about advertising to my father, but an understanding of the nature and use of publicity was something I picked up from friends in public relations and journalism and which I applied to Neiman-Marcus. I recognized the value of a newspaper story, so I attended the fur auctions held at the Fromm silver-fox ranch and in New York, and paid the highest prices for top bundles of skins. These purchases merited local news stories with a picture of me holding up my prize skins, adding to the store's reputation of buying the best wherever it was sold.

When the government announced the lifting of the fifty-seven-year ban on the catching of sea otters, we sent our fur buyer to Seattle to attend the government-sponsored auction with instructions to buy the best bundle, if it was fine enough, at any price. He paid $2300 a skin for the four finest pelts, enough to make one coat. We put the dressed skins on exhibition in the fur department, since most of our customers had never seen a sea-otter skin. Although the animal had been taken off the endangered-species list, we advertised the purchase in a low-key manner, bringing forth a letter of recognition from journalist and author A. C. Greene, who wrote:

Paisano Ranch
Star Route A, Box 874
Austin, Texas 78710

Dear Stanley,

I have been fascinated by the whole sea otter episode and I want to congratulate you on the way Neiman-Marcus handled it—from its dramatic top bid to the exciting but chaste ads which have run as an aftermath. Imagination and curiosity serving are twin virtues of this sort of thing, keeping the public attention to something the public knows very well it will not actually participate in. I think this may be the secret of any great institution which can see beyond the daily greed.

Regards,
A. C. Greene

Unlike politicians whose main concern is the number of letters for or against a proposition, my major interest has always been in the identity and qualifications of the writer. As a goal, I wanted the text in a Neiman-Marcus advertisement to pass the scrutiny of the grammarians among our readers, and the fashion illustrations to please the art critics. All complaints were answered within forty-eight hours, but those coming from persons with special qualifications to complain were given particular management consideration, on the theory that if we could satisfy the most critical of our customers it would be easy to please the balance. Conversely, we believed that if we didn't satisfy the "bell ringers," they would drift away from us and would lead the flock of less discriminating customers with them.

There is no question that our expeditious handling of complaints solidified our reputation for reliability and satisfaction. I am convinced that the speed of reaction to customer dissatisfaction is as important as the final settlement. Establishing a policy of speedy answers and adjustments is easy, but enforcing it requires a hard-nosed management which checks constantly for compliance and refuses to accept excuses for failure to live up to the forty-eight-hour rule.

We were rigorous in maintaining our standards of taste, be it in merchandise, advertising, or other activities in which the store was a participant. This required a certain presumptuousness on my part in setting standards with which some of my associates disagreed at times. I recall an incident in which I criticized our candy buyer for having too large a proportion of her stock in milk chocolate rather than in the dark bittersweet. Her merchandise manager came to her defense arguing, "This is what the public wants. What right do we have to tell them to eat dark chocolate?" I replied, "Milk chocolate is a yokel taste. Chocolate-educated customers will be turned off by seeing so much milk chocolate and we will lose their trade. I'd rather satisfy them than the yokels, if it comes to choosing up sides, but I think we can please both by simply reversing the percentages between the two kinds of chocolate. It's our job to educate our customers as well as to sell them." My directive was followed and eventually our customers switched to the dark chocolate. What the buyer and the merchandise manager had not understood was that our reputation would be endangered when our customers sent Christmas gifts of milk chocolate to sophisticated friends around the country. Both the sender and the store would be blamed; so, in the long run, we did a service for the customers as well as the store.

Our advertising department was always given great creative latitude, but I was adamant that the copy and the art in our advertising be free of vulgarity, either in words or offensive poses. I was critical of hyperbole and extravagant claims that taxed the credibility of our advertising, for I always wanted our readers to believe everything we stated and never to be offended by anything our artists drew. This policy had its difficulties, too, because changing times and fashions bring about changing mores in society, the willingness to accept something today that was taboo yesterday. The problem lies in the fact that the mores change at different rates with different people.

When bikinis became the number one fashion in swimwear, we naturally advertised them—and our sketches showed the figures with navels. One very good customer called me to complain about both our sponsorship of the fashion and the detailed anatomical drawing. I called the matron and told her I should like to come out to discuss the subject with her. Over tea, I explained we were as concerned as she about avoiding vulgarity, but this was a fashion so big, so universal, neither we nor any other store could afford to ignore its existence. I pointed out that what we were really talking about was the absence of ten inches of fabric between the bras and the shorts, which was less than the distance her own skirt had moved upward from 1907 to 1967. I suggested that she was every bit as moral as she was when she wore floor-length skirts. I told her if we refused to carry bikinis, her own granddaughters would insist she take them to another store to shop, and that if we lost the fashion respect of the current generation, we wouldn't have any customers when the older customers passed on. She finally agreed, but said: "At least, you didn't have to show the navels." I explained that we hadn't invented them, and it would be presumptuous for us to try to improve the human body. "How would you answer your

The Building and Preservation of a Mystique

149

granddaughter if she showed you a sketch without a navel and asked you why?" "Neiman-Marcus has meant so much to me and my family," she said, "that I hate to see you doing anything wrong. You have convinced me; you had no alternative."

A complaint like this took time to solve, but its challenge to our standards of taste, reflecting the deep concern of an old and valued customer, was worth the two hours invested in retaining her goodwill. It reaffirmed the Neiman-Marcus reputation for doing things right; reputations, like plaster walls, require constant maintenance.

Not only did we try to keep our reputation in good condition but we made efforts to enhance it constantly. Store life is full of valid, human-interest news stories, but most stores don't capitalize on them. When we opened the store on a Sunday some years ago to outfit a bride and groom who had flown a great distance to shop with us, we tipped off the press (with the customers' consent); when the store had a disastrous fire, we sent out an international news release with full details, getting coverage in newspapers and radio all over the world; when American Airlines had a strike some years ago, stranding fifty-odd stewardesses in Dallas, we gave them temporary jobs and reaped thousands of lines of free publicity.

Our public-relations department was trained to be alert for news happenings outside the store and to capitalize on any story that might have some value for Neiman-Marcus. When Anthony Eden, then British foreign secretary, was visiting the United States in 1952, he lost his homburg hat at a reception. We heard of the loss and wired him that the store was "taking the liberty" of replacing the hat. United Press reported that the new hat arrived by air in time for Eden to wear it to hear the president's State of the Union message, and that Eden had wired me, "Duly touched by your generous gesture and greatly impressed by this typical example of American courtesy. The hat fits as a hat should, and will be a further and constant reminder of my stay in your country." Not only was it a great story for the store and the hat department but I'm confident our customers who read it were proud that their store had made such favorable news.

If a cyclone or a flood hit any community in the Southwest, it was our practice to send a telegram to every charge-account customer in the disaster area, extending our sympathy and willingness to help them or their less fortunate neighbors in any way. We told them, also, that any purchases they needed to make would be billed to them twelve months hence without any carrying charges. Many accepted this offer of extended credit, and not once did we incur an uncollectible account. We did build great public goodwill, which is what public relations is all about.

Many who visit Dallas for the first time, and having heard so much about Neiman-Marcus, are disappointed when they see several undistinguished, cream-colored buildings of mixed styles of architecture. Publicity had conjured a miniature Taj Mahal in their minds. But, once they go through the doors, their spirits are lifted by the feeling of warmth and welcome, by the wide uncluttered aisles and high ceilings, by the quality and design of the fixtures, by the incorporation of paintings and sculpture in the decor. All of this adds up to what the Greeks called "euphoria," a state of well-being. It has been our long-standing conviction that fine merchandise needed to be housed and displayed against a background of fine materials, so we used imported marbles, beautiful wood, and top-quality carpets to create an atmosphere of beauty, not of sumptuousness. These materials, together with the spaciousness we have maintained, create an environment our customers have appreciated. In the newer stores, built since 1956, both exterior and interior architecture have been equally distinguished. We refused to go the more economical but less satisfying route of repeating standardized stores, one like the other. Instead, we have employed distinguished architects, Edward Larrabee Barnes, Gyo Obata, Kevin Roche, and John Carl Warnecke, teaming them up with the interior-design firm founded by the late Eleanor LeMaire, to design individual stores of distinction.

Publicity and beautiful stores are fine, but they are not sufficient to build an enduring reputation in the field of merchandising. The goods must represent honest value, the best available at the various price ranges carried, and the customer service must be superior. Neither of these objectives is accomplished by broad executive directives, but, rather, by painstaking attention to the thousands of details involving both. Retailing, like the operation of hotels, is truly a business of minutiae. A buyer who goes to New York to attend the seasonal apparel showing must visit twenty to thirty showrooms, see three thousand models, select some twenty-five styles from each manufacturer, determine the colors and sizes for each one, write her orders and get home within two weeks, all with the objective of assembling the most authoritative stocks in the land. How wise her judgment was won't be known till the end of the following season, for commitments have to be made from four to six months before the selling period. In addition, she must remember that a very good customer from St. Louis needs a size forty dress to wear to her son's wedding, that a Fort Worth debutante wants a special glamorous dress in pale blue embroidered with delicate silver beading, that she must get expedited delivery on four styles to cover two forthcoming newspaper advertisements, that she must insist that manufacturer X deliver Mrs. Smith's special orders with basted seams for easier alterations, that she must cajole the shipping clerk at manufacturer Y to give her preferential delivery on two current styles for which her salespeople are clamoring.

At any given time, the store will have about 50 percent of its buyers who are skilled professionals, around 30 percent who have two to three years' experience, and the balance are newcomers making their first or second trip to market. This means that the merchandise administrators must not only see the whole market to get a sense of trends but must devote extra time and attention to the neophytes who need the most help. They are taught to look at a dress inside-out to see if the seams are properly bound or pinked, to put their hands in pockets to find out if they are too shallow, to examine colors in the daylight to determine if they look different than in the artificial lights of the showroom. We have always considered it our buyers' responsibility to predigest any merchandise shortcomings rather than to impose that task on our customers. Even with a highly competent staff of buyers, our markdown rods were always loaded—partially with buyers' errors, partially with fashions our customers failed to understand.

Buying fashion merchandise far in advance of the season is not a scientific business; it's a gambling game, at best.

Even while the buying is in progress, and in recent years it has become a twelve-month affair, business must go on. Customers must be served, displays arranged, fashion shows staged, adjustments made, new salespeople trained, recent merchandise arrivals explained, sales enthusiasm maintained. Obviously, there are department heads who oversee these activities, but management must be able to spend an adequate amount of time on the selling floors to detect flaws in the execution of these many jobs, to be the watchful eye that the rank and file of any organization needs and wants.

From the very beginning of the store, management was successful in developing an extraordinary standard of customer service—unsurpassed by any store in the world. When the business was small, the founders trained the sales staff on the selling floor, but as the store grew and multiple units were added, a skilled training department took over that responsibility. New salespeople are taught how to greet customers in a warm, friendly manner; how to find out what the customer is looking for; how to bring the sale to a successful conclusion. They are instructed that "May I help you?" is not the sentence to use when approaching a customer. They are encouraged to start talking about a piece of merchandise that may have stopped the shopper, or to say, "Hello, I'm Dottie Jones. I'll be happy to assist you." Here are the words of counsel given to a class of trainees by Jean Parker, the very able training director of Neiman-Marcus: "Every one of you has been a customer. You have different reasons for buying in different stores from different salespeople. Now you're going to be on the other side of the counter. Don't think for one minute that all the people with whom you will be dealing shop for the same reason. Every customer is an individual."

Like no other store I know, the members of the Neiman-Marcus staff have a great feeling of proprietorship, a keen interest in doing things the "Neiman-Marcus way," a genuine devotion to the interests of the customer as well as the store, a deep respect and pride in the organization of which they are a part. I am more proud of this spirit than any other accom-

The Building and Preservation of a Mystique

153

plishment we may have made, for this, I know, has been of significant importance in building the Neiman-Marcus reputation. I must admit that I am shocked when I receive letters from customers in appreciation of the fact that they were treated so politely when shopping at the store, for when I was growing up in the business, politeness was a necessity and not a virtue.

The annual foreign Fortnight events focused international attention on the store, and the fact that we included a broad spectrum of cultural attractions in addition to dramatic merchandise presentations was the great differential between our promotion and those of other stores which copied us. As a corollary to Jean Parker's admonition that "Every customer is an individual," we recognize that the public has many and varied interests. The bringing of art and musical events, theatrical and literary figures to the Fortnight involves great effort and expense, but they each touch and satisfy different segments of the public, thereby adding to the success of the whole and to the renown of the store.

No one thing that Neiman-Marcus ever did caught the public imagination as much as the Christmas catalogue with its inclusion of unusual, and sometimes fanciful, "His and Her" gifts. In every country I've visited, someone is certain to come up and say, "You're from that store that puts in all those outlandish Christmas gifts." After a number of years of featuring "His and Her" planes, miniature submarines, camels, parachutes, and windmills, our customers have developed the idea that we have everything. It's a nice idea, but hard to live up to. About ten years ago, we featured a full-sized inflatable man, the copy suggesting he would act as a protective companion to women who had to do a lot of night-driving alone. He was a great hit and we sold hundreds of him, but we did disappoint at least one customer, who wrote:

Dear Mr. Marcus:

Thank you for giving my letter your personal attention and for sending me the beautiful Christmas catalogue. Unfortunately, I cannot use your inflatable man, as there are areas in which it would invite aggression rather than provide protection.

I must add that I am a little disappointed, as I had been led to believe that Neiman-Marcus was the one store in America that has—or can provide—everything. Even a colored rubber man.

We were wrong; we should have had the rubber man available in black and brown as well. The customer was correct in calling us down.

It wasn't until long after George Sessions Perry wrote in his book *Texas: A World in Itself,* "Neiman-Marcus is not a store, it is a state of mind or a state of grace," that I really understood what he was trying to say; that was before the word "mystique" had come into popular usage. I've recounted the various factors that went into the building of the Neiman-Marcus reputation: publicity, advertising, merchandise, service. All of these things, over the years, coagulated into a mystique. In many ways it was like a rolling snowball, gathering more and more snow as it gained momentum. The principles to be deduced are: first, you need snow; second, you need a hill; and third, you need someone to give it a push.

A personal mystique has greater durability than corporate ones, for only the possessor can cause bruises or damage. A good individual mystique will follow its owner to the grave. Corporate ones are subject to the hazards from changing managements whose objectives may differ from those who built the mystique, from inexperienced employees who haven't been sufficiently trained in the organization's traditions and methods of operation.

My own personal mystique grew along parallel lines to the Neiman-Marcus mystique. Since I was so closely identified with everything that happened at the store, I was a beneficiary of its successes. As I received trade association awards, decorations from foreign governments, and other recognitions, my status as an authority in fashion and merchandising became a factor in my mystique. My interest in art, music, and education gave my reputation a cultural coloration. Activities in behalf of liberal political candidates and in support of the Bill of Rights drew mixed responses from the public, a large segment of which would prefer that its mercantile leaders be seen and not heard. My willingness to become involved in controversial matters, however, affected my mystique positively as well as negatively. On balance, I think that even those who disagreed with me most violently gave me begrudging credit for sincerity.

A mystique can suffer from dry rot if the original management fails to renew, to keep up-to-date, and it can suffer equally from the growth pains of too hasty expansion. A mystique can act like a ghost; it can come back to haunt you. A customer, disappointed by a defective piece of merchandise or offended by the taste of an advertisement, might very well say, "I would not have expected anything different from another store, but I feel let down that Neiman-Marcus would be so irresponsible."

Whenever an institution or an individual begins to be the subject of amusing jokes, that is evidence of a mystique at work. Forty years ago there were thousands of Ford "Tin Lizzie" tales in circulation. The number of stories involving Neiman-Marcus have been legion throughout the whole Southwest for many years.

There has been a standing gag among many husbands about the mesmerizing effects Neiman-Marcus has had on their wives, so that many of the jokes have been built on that theme. As an example, a wife was commenting on her desire to be cremated on her death. "I want you to promise me cremation," she said, "but since we don't have a crematory in Shreveport, you'll have to send my body to Dallas for cremation." "Well, I'll be darned," replied her spouse, "I didn't know that Neiman-Marcus did that, too." At a homecoming party for Liz Carpenter on her return to Austin from Washington, where she had been Mrs. Lyndon Johnson's press secretary, the *Dallas Times Herald* reported, "A couple of Baptist hymns finished the program at Liz's party, 'Amazing Grace' and 'Love Lifted Me.' It was rousing. 'Actually, I'm an Episcopalian,' Liz said, 'that's a Neiman-Marcus Methodist.'"

If a company's name is used in speech or writing as a

standard, that's evidence of the recognition of the mystique. A shopping center at Westport, Connecticut, ran an advertisement prior to Christmas in 1975 with the headline: WHO NEEDS NEIMAN-MARCUS WHEN THE WOODSHED'S IN WESTPORT? The mystique had traveled some fifteen hundred miles! And then, fifteen hundred miles in the opposite direction, on the West Coast, the *Los Angeles Times* in 1976 published a news story under the heading, "Goodies You Can't Find in a Store," with the following copy, "The Neiman-Marcus catalogue has a reputation as the end-all for elite exotica —but even N-M couldn't match some of the choice goodies offered to more than five hundred black-tie guests last weekend at the Newport Harbor Art Museum's auction." Neiman-Marcus and its famous Christmas catalogues were being used as a standard of measurement.

In the retail business it is an accepted fact of life that a new buyer will have higher markdowns the first season than thereafter, for every buyer uses the proverbial new broom to sweep out the stock purchased by the predecessor—good and bad alike. Something similar occurs when a new top executive enters a business from the outside. In order to lure him away from his previous employment, he has probably been overpaid. If a business is a sick one, then the new executive has to take prompt and radical remedial action, but a healthy institution doesn't require the same treatment. Yet, it often gets it because the new CEO, recognizing he is overpaid, feels impelled to turn things over to justify his salary and to demonstrate that he is the boss.

In any business there are many ways of solving problems that go beyond just the right way and wrong way. There are even right ways and wrong ways of executing the right decision, but they require an intimate knowledge of the historical background of the business, an understanding of both staff and customer attitudes. A new ownership, a new management, is under public suspicion until it has proved its ability, responsibility, and credibility.

Any new management is at a disadvantage until it has passed these tests, whether it be a football coach, a university president, or a new chief executive officer of a store. They are all under similar pressures to win games, balance the budgets, or increase profits; and, in striving to accomplish these objectives rapidly, they are very apt to damage their institutional mystique, if they happen to have one.

Since the mystique is very tough, almost like an old Japanese lacquered tray, having been built up with hundreds of coats of reputation, it can absorb the wounds of immature judgment, the abrasions of ignorance, the shock of crudity, the mishandling by clumsy hands. A mystique can survive abuse for six months or a year or even two, but unless the discriminating sector of the public sees a change forthcoming, it will slowly turn away and concentrate its attention, its support, its purchasing, elsewhere. Once the elite change directions, the others are sure to follow.

Lord & Taylor had a mystique during the days when Dorothy Shaver was its directing head. She created a style of advertising with the distinctive sketches by Hood, an extremely able artist, that personified the type of customer she was striving to serve. Shaver knew the part of the market she wanted; it was the suburban twenty-five- to forty-year-young matron and business woman, on the East Coast; and that's where Lord & Taylor stores were at that time; Shaver never wavered, she never tried to be a Bergdorf, or a Saks; she was Lord & Taylor and built a mystique about the store. When she died, successive managements operated on momentum, but that finally slowed down to the point that Associated Dry Goods, the parent of Lord & Taylor, brought in new management that is solving its problems by building more stores in many markets, with no apparent point of view except to be something to everybody—and nothing particular to anybody. That is a case of a mystique gone to seed. The old one can never be recovered; perhaps a new one can be built.

Bendel's, on West Fifty-seventh Street in New York, was a fine specialty store, with an old distinguished name, that was running on its inner tube when Maxey Jarman of Genesco bought it and brought in Geraldine Stutz, president of the I. Miller shoe division owned by Genesco, to run it. Genesco has done many foolish things in retailing, but it picked a winner in Gerry, despite her limited retail experience. She developed a new concept of what Bendel's should be like and mean to the market, renovated it from top to bottom, and, to Genesco's credit, they backed her all the way, including her idea of making an avenue of little shops within the store. She, like Dorothy Shaver, knew to whom she wanted to cater; in her case it was to be the café society set, the rich New York hippie group, the slim girls wearing sizes four to ten, who would respond to exclusive, avant-garde merchandise. She had a fetish about exclusivity and she had the drive to lead her buyers to develop things that would be found at Bendel's alone. She conceived a small, exclusive business, small enough to be able to change direction quickly, small enough to enable her to have her finger in every merchandise pie in the place. She may not have made much money for Genesco, but she didn't lose any for them, which is more than can be said for many of their retail endeavors. She built a mystique, and she'll be a hard act to follow, unless her successor takes the time to thoroughly understand not only what Gerry Stutz did but why. I guess one of my greatest regrets in retailing is that I never had the opportunity of working with her, for she has taste, enthusiasm, conviction, flair, and a good trading sense.

A mystique grew around Adam Gimbel and Saks Fifth Avenue, for he brought modernity, the twentieth century, to Fifth Avenue. He was a good-looking, charming, gregarious bachelor, and he had his own mystique. He looked like a Latin lover, he played polo, shot grouse in Scotland and ducks in Cuba, played bridge on the New Jersey shore, and he had *style*. Adam took over the direction of Saks Fifth Avenue when Gimbels acquired Saks after the death of Horace Saks, the founder. He filled the store with large assortments of exclusive merchandise from Europe as well as the United States. He installed custom-shirt and clothing departments, a salon for made-to-order dresses. He built the dominant fine shoe business in the country. He believed that large stocks, in bad times and good, were necessary to give his customers proper assortments from which to select, remarking, "We can always make dollars, but we can't always make customers; I would rather lose dollars than lose customers." The stocks at Saks were always noteworthy for their sheer size, but they were characterized by great unevenness in quality and taste between departments. Some, like their men's departments, showed a consistent standard of taste. Others, like their very successful handbag department, showed no evidence of any editing. It was full of the good, bad, and indifferent. Nor was he ever able to overcome the rudeness and disinterestedness of his New York sales staff, probably because he was more concerned with merchandise and store architecture than with customer service.

Adam was the first to go completely national with full-sized specialty stores, extending the Saks operation to Chicago and the West Coast. A few years after his death, the Gimbel business, including its brightest star, Saks Fifth Avenue, was sold to Brown and Williamson Tobacco, a subsidiary of British-American Tobacco, which to all outside appearances never fully comprehended the Saks mystique. They retained one of Adam's protégés, Allan Johnson, as chairman of the board and CEO, but brought in Bob Suslow, a tough, successful volume-producer, as president and general-merchandise manager to achieve immediate increase in sales and profits. Suslow subsequently was elevated to the top job when Johnson was moved over to the corporate offices.

Suslow's slam-bang department-store techniques apparently have given the store the improved operating results wanted by the British ownership, but in the course of accomplishments the Saks mystique has been severely wounded, probably beyond recovery.

They have plans to add eighteen more stores in the next ten years to give them a billion dollars in sales and, if that comes off, there is no way, in my opinion, that Saks can maintain its position as one of the top-quality specialty stores of the world. That much volume will corrode the buyers' mentalities; they will think big, not fine.

The building of any corporate mystique presupposes a competent management that has a clear understanding of its direction and the public which it is serving; the perpetuation of such a mystique requires similar competence. Unfortunately, the expansion rate in the specialty-store field far exceeded its ability or willingness to grow a sufficient number of specialty-store merchants with all-around qualifications, forcing it to go to the department stores for leadership. For the most part, these men, good as they may be on balance-sheet performance, have little understanding of the nuances of specialty-store operation. A lapse of taste in a department store is a one-day wonder; in a specialty store, a *gaucherie* can cause the loss of a $100,000 sable-coat sale.

When experienced management is thin, supervision suffers, as demonstrated in two incidents that occurred at Neiman-Marcus. One involved a product named "Jesus jeans," which a new buyer bought and which escaped the scrutiny of management. Only when the Roman Catholic Archdiocese in New York raised a complaint, did the store's CEO learn about this bit of tastelessness and order the removal of the product from stock. This dented the mystique, but didn't crush it. When the "punk" fashion was imported from London (a questionable fashion and merchandising decision), the buyer requested windows for the clothes. A young display director, left on his own while his superiors were in another city opening a new Neiman-Marcus store, decided to give it the full treatment with garbage cans and other "punk" props. That would have been bad enough, but he added to his bad judgment by showing the clothes on new hairless, black window mannequins, drawing an immediate and justifiable protest from a few leaders of the black community. The *Dallas Morning News,* in reporting the incident, wrote, "Black is not beautiful when it is bald and punky, accented by garbage and displayed in a window of one of the country's elite stores, according to black activist Al Lipscomb. Neiman-Marcus has removed a display from its downtown store window that featured four black, bald mannequins outfitted in 'punk' fashion and in a setting of high- and low-class garbage. . . ." And Neiman-Marcus said, "Enough, we goofed." The store reacted properly and quickly, but any repeated departures from good taste and propriety can explode its mystique.

The mystique of a fine store can rub off on its executives, making them look very desirable to competition searching for new talent. Neiman-Marcus, in this way, has supplied the CEOs of a dozen or more companies around the nation. Some have made it, others have failed. Mystique is not portable, and, for that reason, Neiman-Marcus does not extend the same guarantee on its executives as it does on its merchandise.

*The Building
and
Preservation
of a
Mystique*

161

A healthy mystique might be likened to a compartmentalized balloon; both can take a great deal of abuse, both can survive nicks, bruises, cuts, and gashes, up to a certain point. After enough compartments are perforated, the balloon will lose buoyancy and fall to the ground, and so will a mystique. But there the comparison ends; the balloon can be patched up and reinflated, but I don't know of any fallen mystique that has ever been restored. Theoretically, it should be possible; but it would require the same long years of reputation-building it took in the first place, perhaps more because a bad reputation would have to be overcome. I just don't believe any individual or corporation would have the staying power to accomplish it. So, if you are fortunate to have a good mystique, be faithful to it and treat it with understanding and care.

Habit de Chapellier

A Paris Chez N de Larmessin Rue St Jacques à la Pôme d'Or.   Avec Privil du Roy

10

Putting the Catalogue to Bed

A Christmas catalogue of the type Neiman-Marcus originated presents an interesting case study of the search for quality merchandise covering a wide range of prices, from $10 to $100,000, which will stimulate at least 10 percent of the one million worldwide recipients to fill out order blanks and put them in the mail. With an ever-increasing investment in catalogue production and distribution, currently well over $1 million, the book must pay off in terms of dollar volume to justify such an expenditure.

Although the sales achievements are vital, there are other important considerations as well. The million people who get the book and the two and a half million who read it have only one thing in common: they are either Neiman-Marcus charge customers, who receive it gratis, or would-be customers who have paid $2 for the catalogue. This charge was originated to discourage frivolous requests from the thousands of people who write in for anything free. The book is the only mailing of the year which goes to all active Neiman-Marcus customers, and must, therefore, carry the message of Neiman-Marcus merchandise superiority in a manner representative of the traditions of the company. The aesthetics of the book become of paramount importance to transmit the Neiman-Marcus image. Finally, since the catalogue generates a vast amount of national and foreign publicity, it must contain bona fide newsworthy items to merit broad press coverage.

It is easy to create a catalogue to be sent to a selective list of silver or porcelain collectors, or polo players, hunters, and fishermen, but it is infinitely more difficult to do one that covers such a broad variety of gifts for all ages, for men, women, and children who live in all the climate zones, at prices which are affordable by those with modest incomes as well as by the wealthy, and all in a quality standard representing the best in its class. From an institutional aspect, Neiman-Marcus can't afford to catalogue an item inconsistent with its reputation for fashion, quality, and value. There is no margin for error, for the discriminating customers of the world are looking on. From a purely economic view, the company could not afford to take a knowing risk on an item of even questionable quality out of concern for customer dissatisfaction, horrendous returns, and loss of profitability. Buyers may be willing to accept mediocrity from other stores, but when the article comes from Neiman-Marcus, they will accept no compromises. The military have a description for those who rise in ranks: "The higher you climb on the totem pole, the more your tail shows"—or words to that effect! That's one of the prices of success.

In 1977, the Christmas catalogue marked the fiftieth year of publication. For the first thirty years the catalogues were nicely printed but undistinguished presentations of gift assortments aimed at reminding customers that Christmas was coming and Neiman-Marcus was waiting and ready to serve them. There was no visible effort to encourage mail-order shopping.

In the mid-1950s, as the European markets began to flourish, we started to amplify our selections with imaginative articles we could buy for exclusive distribution. In the spring of 1956, I, with a few buyers, made a trip covering Europe from Italy to Scandinavia, picking up three or four unique gifts from each country. We then went to Holland, where we had a special full-color catalogue supplement printed by the historic printing house of Enchedé & Zohnen. It was shipped by boat to the port of Houston, where a dock strike held up the cargo for weeks, almost causing us to miss Christmas distribution. The results were gratifying, though we decided never again to have a seasonal mailer printed out-side the United States. This book proved to management and buyers alike that we could sell more expensive merchandise through the mails than we had thought possible.

In that catalogue we introduced, for the first time, an Italian stainless-steel man's pocketknife with a single blade, a file, and a folding pair of scissors at $2.95! We received two thousand orders and were forced to fly in the reorder of one thousand pocketknives to avoid disappointing the customers who had ordered them for gifts. We also featured a set of six French steel steak knives with wooden handles at $6.95, which were far superior in quality to the domestically made knives we had previously sold at higher prices. These two items have become perennials and have appeared in almost every Neiman-Marcus Christmas book in the ensuing years, although the prices have risen to $12.50 for the man's pocket-knife and to $22.50 for the steak knives. The catalogue cover that year was designed by Ludwig Bemelmans, the author and artist, and began the Neiman-Marcus tradition of com-missioning catalogue covers by distinguished artists. Not only did we get more exciting covers but, for the first time, we also picked up national press coverage on them.

The following year, our man's buyer found a handsome tool chest in a burl walnut cabinet made by Asprey of Lon-don in their own workshops. It had to retail for $550, an extravagant price at that time. He called me from London to get approval of it, saying that he had bought two of them. Sight unseen, but on the basis of his enthusiasm, I authorized him to buy a dozen. We received orders for twenty-five, ten more than Asprey was able to supply. In the same catalogue we illustrated a sterling-silver thimble decorated with semi-precious stones, which I had found by accident in Florence when I was shopping for silver punch bowls. I have a habit when visiting showrooms to poke around the shelves and look into cupboards. That's how I happened to find the thimbles which had been stored away. The silversmith didn't even want to make them anymore but, based on our punch-bowl purchase, he agreed to accept the thimble order. It retailed for $2.50, proving to be one of the most successful items we had ever marketed. They were fine enough to send to a grandmother or a duchess, and, as a matter of fact, one was sent as a gift to a reigning princess.

When I told this story to a friend, he remarked, "That was a case of serendipity." I had a vague recognition of the word, which I knew was coined by the writer Horace Walpole in the eighteenth century, but I wasn't completely clear as to its exact meaning. I went to my library and found an article in a medical journal, edited by Dr. William B. Bean, in which he quoted a Walpole letter in a book by Theodore G. Remer, *Serendipity and the Three Princes.* Remer reprinted a letter in which Walpole first used the word "serendipity." He wrote, "I once read a silly fairy tale, called *The Three Princes of Serendip:* as their Highnesses travelled, they were always making discoveries, by accident and sagacity, of things which they were not in quest of: for instance, one of them discovered that a mule blind of the right eye had travelled the road lately, because the grass was eaten only on the left side, where it was worse than on the right—now do you understand *serendipity?*"

Dr. Bean went on to editorialize, "Serendipity, thus, immediately is defined as the gift of finding, by chance and by sagacity, valuable or agreeable things not sought for. It is not an 'either/or' phenomenon, but both accident and sagacity have to come in while one is in the pursuit of something else. Thus 'accidental discovery' is not a synonym for serendipity." In other words, discoveries occur when you are looking for something—with your eyes wide open—a lesson I have tried to teach to executive trainees.

In 1957, Saul Steinberg was persuaded to design the Christmas-catalogue cover and gift-wrapping paper, although he subsequently found himself unhappy over the fact that his designs were being torn as the gifts were opened, which I deeply regretted, for I like to respect the wishes and sensitivities of any artist we commission. As a consolation, I explained that many customers were buying gifts with the request that the paper be delivered to them in a roll which they then had framed.

We were making progress in encouraging buyers to do more creative work in the markets which became evident in the 1958 catalogue. The fur stole was at the height of popularity that year, and the fur buyers had one of our shops make an ombré mink stole, shading from a pecan brown to beige and using six different natural colors in the process. This marked the first departure from the use of mink in other than the conventional solid colors, a trend that accelerated in following years. The glove buyer came up with the most ingenious idea of the season. While she was working on her glove purchase, Roger Faré, the distinguished French glovemaker, showed her the thinnest ostrich skins that had ever been tanned. "Why, they are so thin, you could stuff one in a walnut shell," he exclaimed. She immediately proceeded to get some large French walnuts and stuffed them with the gloves. The concept was so appealing to our customers that she found herself stuffing walnuts all the month of December to fill the demand which this fresh idea had created.

Topping a great success story in successive years is tough, but we did so the next year when one of our executives came up with the "His and Her" Beechcraft planes. That story was picked up internationally as well as in the domestic press, and we were besieged with phone calls from foreign papers and television. As a backup page, just in case "His and Hers" didn't work, we featured a desert-island scene with a complete set of the Modern Library, some 304 regular-size books plus 80 giants, for $828.80. There was another thought behind the second page, as well. We figured that if one paper grabbed the "His and Her" story, we'd have something else for the competing paper to write about. That worked, too.

Picking the concepts for the big-idea pages is not easy; some years we've succeeded and other years we've bombed, but on balance I think Neiman-Marcus has had a fine batting average. Some ideas sound good in the conversational stage, but don't materialize well; some get poor execution in photography and presentation, others lose their charm in print. The big-idea page must, above all, have originality, like the Chinese junks in 1962 and the "His and Her" camels in 1967; it must have wit as well as humor; and, above all, it must be in good taste—and, incidentally, it has been in this last area of qualifications that most of the imitators of the big-idea page have gone astray. However incongruous the idea may be, it must always have a slight degree of plausibility that makes the reader ask the question, "I wonder if they really will sell one of those?"

Producing a Neiman-Marcus Christmas catalogue must be something like producing a movie. It goes into the selection process in early June when a staff consisting of the mail-order director, the sales manager, the general-merchandise manager, the fashion director, the copy chief, the art director, the production manager, the photographic supervisor, the budget controller, and the final boss—the president—all meet with the one-hundred-odd buyers and the fifteen divisional merchandise managers to look at the samples the buyers have selected from all over the world as their proposals for representations in the book.

Some buyers have a keen perception of what is both new and salable; others are burdened with historic memories of what sold in previous years and bring up rehashes of former successes; others haven't the slightest idea what it's all about. Each member of the judging committee has a particular concern: the mail-order director must look for overall sales performance; the general-merchandise manager is looking for departmental balance, since the stores are required to carry representation of all catalogue merchandise; the fashion director is judging the fashion rightness of the presentations; the art director is wondering how to get all of the diverse items into pleasing and selling layouts; the photographic supervisor worries whether specific items can be photographed well in the colors submitted; the budget controller wonders if there is enough vendor-money participation to keep his budget in equilibrium; the sales manager is analyzing what contribution each item is making to the total impact; the copy chief is concerned with the adequacy of information from which to produce copy on schedule; the production manager wants to know when she will get final corrected samples; and the boss is listening to all of these considerations, in addition to acting as the final arbiter on them as well as on taste and adherence to quality standards.

The attainment of merchandise balance is a major objective, and is accomplished only after severe probing and analysis. Is there sufficient variety in gifts from $5 to $20?

Are the cosmetic items overweighing the book? When the apparel items are gathered together, do they all look alike? Are there enough sweaters, or too many? Will the necktie selection appeal to a broad enough range in tastes, that is, for solids, stripes, bold and conservative patterns? In the desire to feature new fashion trends, have some of the classics been ignored? Is there a robe to fulfill a grandmother's requirements? For a young mother? For a college girl? Are there any gifts to send to a family? Are there an adequate number of impersonal gifts which a man can send his secretary? Are there sufficient novelties to entice the most sophisticated buyers? Are there any surefire sellers that can be depended on to produce exceptional sales? Any moderate-priced universal sort of gift that will act as an "order starter"? Have expensive gifts been properly represented? These are but a few of the hundreds of test questions that must be answered before the selections can be considered as final and the catalogue put into production.

No wonder the selection meetings, which go on for two weeks, are traumatic and leave buyers and merchandise managers with wounded feelings and bruised egos. Decisions are made either by consensus or by the most senior voices present. Invariably, after all selections have been completed, a few items drop out because of unavailability. Invariably, after the book is printed, several manufacturers have fires or floods or other calamities that prevent them from making delivery. Trying to guess the number of orders which will be received on each of the four hundred and fifty items, and in what colors and sizes, is like trying to guess the number coming up on a roulette wheel. If you don't order enough, you will disappoint the customers; if you order too many, you'll be stuck with the residue, and even the best gift of the season doesn't have much value in a stock after Christmas. Despite all of the problems of selection, and forecasting, Neiman-Marcus ends up with less than 7 percent of orders which have to be canceled for lack of availability.

I found at one time there was a reluctance to include expensive gifts, for their sales predictability was less than for popularly priced articles. To protect the store's reputation, I instituted a section called "The Incomparables" and reserved four pages for the gifts which could be described, "than which there is nothing finer." Price was no consideration so long as the quality and taste would satisfy the most discriminating wealthy customer. Interestingly enough, these items sold, but since many were unique, we were unable to fill multiple orders.

To be sure that we didn't forget the gadget-seekers and those who wanted fun gifts, I instituted a page which we named "Things You Never Knew You Needed Until Now." On this page went such greatly needed things as a live armadillo, a bulletproof vest, worry beads, an eleven-foot pole for things you wouldn't touch with a ten-foot pole. We received lots of orders and we hope we gave lots of laughs.

We strived to give the catalogue a light touch; we spoofed ourselves a bit, to make the task of going through the book more enjoyable. We did a page of "lucky" gifts, consisting of items considered lucky in their country of origin, such as a shamrock pillbox, cuff links engraved with the Chinese symbols of good luck, an evil eye used to ward off evil spirits, a *Tasset el Rabah* copper bowl with spinning fish from Lebanon, and the hand of Fatima made in the Arab section of Jerusalem. My brother Edward conceived a "growing" gift for children with things that grew fast enough to capture their imagination, like a baby elephant, a Galápagos turtle, and Peruvian corn, which shot up to fifteen or twenty feet in height. We sold one elephant at $500, fob Dallas, five turtles, and thousands of packets of corn.

We exposed our customers to the most unusual products from the world's markets and from the fertile imagination of a very talented group of buyers and merchants. We originated the full-length, white ermine bathrobe lined with terry cloth, selling three of them to customers in California, New York, and Illinois; we suggested "look-alike sculptures, or stand-ins," inspired by the hit mystery play of 1971, *Sleuth*, which were great on the stage but flops in the catalogue. We designed a bed sheet imprinted with hundreds of little sheep for insomniacs to count off to get to sleep; in 1969, we foresaw the coming of the personalized home data processor by showing a Honeywell kitchen computer programmed with recipes of the famous Helen Corbitt; we offered eight-foot-long Quivut scarves, weighing four ounces, hand-knitted by the Eskimos from the underwool of the musk-ox, the numerous orders for which created a minor labor crisis in the Arctic regions; for $5,000, we presented a pair of narwhal tusks, mounted in tole stands, which went to a New Orleans collector whose order was the first of twenty-three received; "His and Her" manuscript letters by George and Martha Washington, sold to a dealer; a stop-and-go silver-plated gravy and condiment electric train for a large dining-room table, copied from an original commissioned in the nineteenth century by an Indian rajah; and, in 1977, a limited-edition scarf, a reproduction of a Raoul Dufy water-color, at $180, and the original at $18,000, resulting in a near sellout of the scarf and the sale of the painting.

Inspirations came from many places, many sources. I read or skimmed over a hundred magazines a month to keep up with what was going on in different fields of activity and thought. Occasionally, I'd pick up a new product idea, but more often a photograph would spark off a completely unrelated idea. Such a brainstorm occurred once when I was reading the Sunday comics, of which I am a great devotee, and saw a cartoon of a Halloween skeleton. "Why not make a full-size, soft skeleton, so that those who don't have a skeleton in the closet will be able to buy one or, at least, send one to some other unfortunate?" The trouble was to find a maker, but finally my daughter-in-law, Heather Marcus, a talented designer and producer in her own right, came to the rescue and made it up. It was submitted for the 1977 Christmas catalogue, but it was difficult to find the appropriate departmental location for it. Finally, the toiletry buyer figured she could put sachets in its padding and thereby qualify it for the fragrance shop, where it had a great success.

But so much for the successes; we've had our failures, too. Our nineteenth-century brass Newmarket jockey scales at $2500 didn't get a nibble, fortunately, for they are now worth $8500 and we have withdrawn them from sale, reserving them for display purposes; "Peruna," a child's galloping horse from Spain, developed mechanical lameness and we had to take back the one hundred and fifty we had sold; a golfer's caddy, operated electronically by voice command, was never delivered by its maker, forcing us to cancel with embarrassment the several hundred orders received; a Chinese opal snuff bottle, at $2000, which we described in the catalogue as eighteenth-century—for which several dozen collectors promptly rebuked us, asserting that it was nineteenth-century, and although the purchaser accepted our apologies she refused to send it back for credit; a jet-powered glider that was not certificated by the FAA until after both Christmas and our prospective buyer were long gone; a dinosaur safari with a guarantee of a dinosaur skeleton for presentation to a museum, which was sold but never paid for because of subsequent financial difficulties of the customer; and finally, the N-Bar-M mouse ranch in lucite, which made me wince every time I saw it reported on television, for it had a built-in repulsiveness, which we didn't recognize until we saw it in print.

Obviously, the Neiman-Marcus catalogue has had its critics who have disparaged it on the grounds that it offered a lot of expensive things that people didn't or shouldn't want. On the other hand, it has not only been commercially successful but has won its share of advertising kudos and favorable editorial comment. It has probably become the single most sought-after Christmas catalogue in the world, earning more international attention than any other published in the United States. It has proved that fashionable and expensive merchandise can be sold by mail, just as, at an earlier date, Sears and others had demonstrated that its customers would buy clothing and household staples from a catalogue. Its success has changed the direction of mail-order marketing of better goods, and has encouraged a host of imitators attempting to cash in on a winning formula. The catalogue has now become a collector's item: a copy of the 1942 edition recently sold for $90.

Several years ago when my wife and I were in London attending the queen's garden party, Earl Mountbatten saw us in the crowd and presented us to Her Majesty, Queen Elizabeth. He then escorted us around to present us to other members of the royal family. When we came to Princess Alexandra, who had visited Dallas to open a British Fortnight officially, she exclaimed, "I'm angry at you. I didn't receive my Neiman-Marcus Christmas catalogue this past year." Fortunately, we can always pass the blame to the postal service.

The ultimate proof of recognition occurs when a name or product is used in a work of fiction. Richard Condon performed this act of canonization in *Bandicoot:*

... he found Captain Huntington breakfasting on the sheltered fantail of the ship, ... chewing daintily from an enormous *saucisse de veau* cooked with shallots in butter, sipping tea, and reading volume H–K of *Grove's Dictionary of Music.* Steinitt had packed the Captain's favorite dictionaries; his Beerbohm, his Firbanks, and his Neiman-Marcus catalogue knowing well that anyone might tire of sex, but never of the masters.

I'll settle for that literary company, anytime!

Habit de Malletier Coffretier

A Paris Chez N. de L'Armessin Rue S.t Jacques a la Pomme d'Or

Avec Privil du Roy

11

Traveling Abroad

In the almost forty years since the war I've made over fifty trips to Europe, to the Orient, and two around the world, but not once have I ever gone strictly for pleasure. That doesn't mean that I haven't had fun along the way, but my journeys were essentially for the purpose of searching out the best and newest merchandise in all of the markets of the world. Travel schedules have been tight with many one-night stops, but I have been rewarded by the satisfaction of finding articles or ideas which made the strenuous efforts worthwhile. Retailing is all-encompassing in its scope, and even when I would take off a week to visit a resort, I would either run across a locally made article in one of the shops which I had to track down to its source, or I would meet customers or vendors with whom I felt obligated to have a drink or a meal.

Since 1957, the date of our first foreign Fortnight, most of my foreign trips were made in behalf of those events. It gave me the opportunity of studying a score of countries in depth. In all candor, I am not positive whether I invented the foreign Fortnights to exhibit and sell the best merchandise of the participating country or whether I did so to have a valid excuse for spending four to six weeks every year in a different country doing an intensive research job. The promotion proved so successful that it has become an annual Neiman-Marcus event since its inception and it gave me an understanding of the various countries in a manner I would never have gained otherwise.

With the sponsorship of the governments, as coproducers, I had entrée to the top political leaders, chiefs of government bureaus, heads of industry, museum and theater directors, and artists. My search was for the best their country had to offer, and not once did the VIPs refuse my invitation to suggest what they believed to be their areas of superiority. I didn't always find them right, but I did pick up some leads I might have otherwise missed. The wives of former ambassadors to the United States were particularly helpful, for they knew from comparative shopping how their countries' products compared with ours.

I met and received assistance from a wide and disparate group of personalities, including: Lord Louis Mountbatten; Brigitte Bardot; Bruno Kreisky, the then foreign minister and now chancellor of Austria; Alberto Giacometti, the artist; Chanoine Kir, one of the French resistance leaders; Josef Stummvoll, librarian of the Bibliothek National of Vienna; Jacques Chaban-Delmas, president of the Chambre des Députés; Captain Terrence O'Neill, prime minister of Northern Ireland; five successive premiers of Italy, none of whom held office for more than three days; Antonio Ghiringhelli, impresario of La Scala; Louise de Vilmorin, the charming and talented poet and novelist; and Savignac, the great French poster artist. Many of them subsequently came to Dallas to participate in the opening activities of the Fortnight.

One of the features of the Fortnight was the commissioning of a poster by a distinguished graphic artist of the country. I told the Comité des Foires in Paris that since we were in search of the best merchandise, I wanted to invite Savignac to design it. They agreed and arranged for me to meet him. I carefully explained to Savignac the nature of our event and the ideas I had developed to symbolize the intercountry solidarity and to memorialize the fact that the French flag had once flown over Texas. Savignac listened patiently and then made an incisive remark I've never forgotten: "Mr. Marcus, what you have told me is very interesting, but to express all of that I should have to compose an essay in the form of a mural. Remember, a poster is a telegram whose objective is to get a message across quickly and intelligibly to people who may be on the move as they see it." The lesson was not lost on me, for I applied Savignac's observation in evaluating every other poster submitted for my approval.

The quality of services in Europe has been affected by many of the same forces as in the United States, namely, prosperity, inflation, and labor shortages. Thanks to jet aircraft, Europe has enjoyed the greatest tourist traffic in history which has taxed all of its facilities. First came the Americans, then the Germans, followed by the Japanese, and now the Middle Easterners. The first three nationalities simply filled the airports, hotels, theaters, and shops, where they bought gifts to take home. The Middle Easterners have done all those things, but, in addition, they have bought up everything in sight, including hotels, flats, and business enterprises.

It has become commonplace to talk about the Americanization of Europe, but in today's world of rapid communications we are importing about as many ideas as we export. We're glad about the modernization of hotel plumbing, we're sad about the proliferation of advertising signs in public places; we are glad when we find taxi drivers who speak English, we're sad that the women no longer wear their picturesque native costumes in Brittany; we're glad that the countries have become more democratic, we're sad about the disappearance of royal titles, which invariably impressed us because we have none. Good food is better in Britain than formerly, poorer in Italy, excellent as ever in France and Switzerland, and about the same in Germany, where it was never distinguished. Service in restaurants has deteriorated as labor shortages have necessitated the employment of immigrants from Malta, Crete, and Greece. There is nothing wrong with waiters from these or any other countries, but they lack the long training and tradition of service that comes from working in the same restaurant for twenty years. Americans who have been spoiled by several decades of favorable exchange rates find prices abroad exorbitant, which means that they are about the same as in the United States for comparable quality. This state of price parity is very distressing to most of us.

Those who complain about the difficulties of travel these days, with the problems of delayed flights, airline strikes, control-tower slowdowns, or mix-ups in reservations, either have forgotten or never knew that there were similar snarls in those leisurely days of luxury-ship ocean travel. Voyages were canceled or delayed when a ship's hull became damaged on a reef, passengers had to handle their own luggage during longshoremen strikes, storms at sea broke both the ships' china and the passengers' arms, and work stoppages on the boat trains from Paris to Cherbourg put travelers in a quandary of how to get themselves and their suitcases and trunks from Paris to the port—some 324 kilometers away.

Whenever the subject of boat-train strikes come up, I always think of an experience my mother had when faced with that situation some years ago. She was then in her early seventies and was traveling with her sister, a few years younger. They had a great deal of luggage, too much to be packed in a car, so she decided to hire a truck to transport her sister, herself, and the bags and the trunks to Cherbourg. On her return, she told about their journey by truck, saying: "I couldn't help but reflect, on that long drive, how each of my four sons might have solved the problem in different ways. If Stanley had been with us, he would have put in a call immediately to some high state official, who would have sent government cars with the compliments of the République de France; if Eddie had been there, he would have thought nothing of asking some of his close friends to drive us as a personal favor; if it had been Herb, the spender, he would have phoned the limousine service to send over a fleet of Rolls-Royces; if Lawrence, the frugal, had been faced with the decision, he would have suggested that we stay in Paris until the strike was over and charge the cost of our accommodations to the steamship line." Mother was very proud of her sons, but she knew them well.

I have been fortunate in that I have been able to stay in the so-called best hotels as I have traveled and I have become accustomed to the services and amenities provided by such hotels. Once in a while, when I have felt the need to retrench, I've taken the least expensive accommodation in them in preference to taking a better room in a lesser hotel. As the result of frequent and sometimes constant travel, I believe that I could qualify for a job as an inspector for the *Guide Michelin*. These are my personal requirements for any hotel I patronize regularly: it should be located within walking distance to the better shopping district; it should have a quiet lobby, the Peninsula in Hong Kong excepted; the rooms should be clean and well-maintained, with clean carpets and no peeling paint on walls, ceilings, or windowsills; prompt room service; night maid service; simple decoration; and a pleasant ambiance. For these qualities, I am willing to pay top price.

A good restaurant at my hotel is nice but not necessary, for I prefer to dine out at the many good restaurants in metropolitan cities. I appreciate the mark of hospitality of a bouquet of fresh flowers and/or a bottle of champagne on arrival, with the full knowledge, of course, that the cost is included in the room rate. The Bristol in Paris, where I have stayed for thirty years, has never complimented me with even a single *muguet* boutonniere, the traditional flower used to celebrate the first of May in France. When I first started staying there, immediately after the war, they didn't supply bars of soap. I complained to the son of the manager, saying: "At your prices you certainly should be able to provide soap as other hotels all over the world do." He shook his head and replied, "My father is a very conservative man. He thinks that only brothels give free soap." The following year when I returned, I was pleased to find a bar of soap, small as it was, in the bathroom.

In general, I prefer to stay in a well-cared-for, older hotel than a brand-new chain hotel, whose staff hasn't had the time to settle down any more than their wine. It takes years for a fine piece of furniture to develop a patina; a hotel is no different. The jets not only revolutionized transportation but they had the same effect on hotels, even the best ones. Travelers who used to go to London for twelve days now spend an average of three, which means that the management has to fill the hotel four times to maintain the same occupancy rate.

This rapid turnover shifts the emphasis from managing the hotel, with all of its problems, to being a sales promoter to get business. The guests formerly stayed long enough for the staff to get to know them and to learn their tastes, but now they move so fast it's difficult to render personalized service. And, to make matters even worse, the staff turns over almost as fast as the guests.

If I receive any publicity on my arrival in a European city, I am immediately besieged by phone calls and letters from all sorts of people who have something to sell. As a result of the Christmas-catalogue fame, everyone who has a castle, a collection of paintings, or a lock of Lafayette's hair pounces on me.

One phone call led to the acquisition of the entire stock of a distinguished antique dealer; another to the purchase of a collection of museum-quality, seventeenth-century, lace-trimmed handkerchiefs; and another to a privately owned group of Chinese court robes, which we bought and promptly sold to a man who donated them to the Metropolitan Museum. Perhaps one out of a hundred offerings work out to be of interest, but one good buy can compensate for the time invested in examining the balance.

When I first went to Europe on buying trips, our sources of merchandise supply depended on what our buying offices had brought in to show us and what we discovered ourselves by pounding the pavements and looking into the boutique windows. Europe always had great merchandise fairs organized around certain merchandise classifications—like toys, housewares, and watches—but now there are fairs for many more products, such as ready-to-wear, piece-goods, and gifts. This makes it easier for buyers to see the large spectrum of the market availability and to determine which lines should be further investigated. The fairs are vast, crowded, and confusing, but timesaving. I recall a visit to a fair in Osaka, Japan, which covered almost ten acres with thousands of products of no interest to me, but I dutifully walked through the entire exhibition, coming up with but one item, a lacquered metal strongbox which sounded an alarm when opened. We featured it as a boy's gift in the catalogue with such success that it was repeated for five years, eventually producing over $100,000 in sales.

There are so many fairs held in all parts of the world that a buyer could be away from home all year just covering them. Since this is not practical, a store has to determine which are the most important ones for the buyers to see and which can be viewed by the foreign buying offices which issue detailed reports and evaluations. Most stores in the United States send their buyers to some of the fairs; but, now, in order to service those who don't go to Europe, they're sending mini-fairs to New York and other markets.

The development of the fair has been one of the most dramatic changes in European marketing. The other visible change I have noticed is the disappearance of bargains in the antique and secondhand markets. There was a time when a private or store buyer could visit the flea markets and small antique shops and come up with wonderful buys, but no longer is that likely to happen. The supply of goods has dried up to a trickle, and with the demand as great as ever, prices have skyrocketed.

Despite its postwar industrialization and the flight of labor from handwork, Europe still offers many facilities, still relatively small in size, which have the capacity to produce the finest of many types of consumer goods. One good example is a shop like Peter on the Faubourg Saint-Honoré; it has not yielded to the dishwasher age, still makes and sells cutlery of the finest quality, which must be washed by hand. As a specialist in articles made of steel, it knows which country produces the appropriate steel for specific usage: Sweden for scissors; France for steak knives; Germany for stainless. With the introduction of new alloys, such as titanium and molybdenum, steel is an example of a product that is better today than it was fifty years ago. A hair tweezer in its leather sheath from Peter is a joy to possess.

Despite the vicissitudes of Italian politics and the frequency of strikes, Italian industry continues to weather its problems, comes forth with fresh new merchandise ideas, maintains its standards of quality, and delivers its orders on time. For reasons not entirely clear to me, the Italians have been able to deal with the consequences of inflation better than the other European countries; prices have increased, but within reasonable limits. The individual craftsmen may have disappeared, but the spirit of fine craftsmanship has been retained by small factories, where there is still a willingness to make something special for the customer. I had such an experience a few years ago when I was visiting the factory of Savanelli, the pipemaker.

As Mr. Savanelli was showing me his line, I absentmindedly played with a soft pipe stem which had not yet been baked. I glanced at it and saw that I had molded the upper half of the letter *S*, which I showed to Mr. Savanelli and asked him to bake for me. He shook his head negatively, saying, *"Che pazzia,"* which in English translates to "That's crazy." I told him I would pay for it and to go on and bake it. I started smoking it and every pipe-smoker who saw it wanted one. We ordered the pipe for stock and put it in the Christmas catalogue under the headline, "The Chairman's Pipe." Over a period of five years we've sold thousands of them, and Mr. Savanelli no longer thinks the idea is *pazzia*. The nicest thing about the story is that he has refused to sell the pipe to any other customers, recognizing that it was my idea. Such manufacturer loyalty is unusual in any language.

Without Europe as a source of supply, the United States would be poverty-stricken for fine fabrics made from wool, cotton, silk, and linen; for our domestic production of natural-fiber, luxury cloths is negligible. We depend on Italy, Spain, Germany, and Britain for the best leather tannage and fine leather articles, from shoes to handbags. The best plated silver still comes from Britain, and the finest porcelain and earthenware are imported from Britain, Italy, and France. In the past few years, European ready-to-wear has become a strong competitor to our garment industry, which previously had no foreign rivalry of significance. The whole explanation lies in Europe's ability to make a variety of better things in small enough quantities to give an interesting diversity to U.S. retail stocks. This may prove to be a temporary advantage that could disappear if the Common Market fosters larger economic units of production and discourages the competition provided by the thousands of medium-size factories.

This comment is frequently heard: "Well, Europe isn't like it used to be." Of course it isn't, but neither is the United States. Change is the only constant force in life; some of it is for the better, some for the worse. Legislation or hand-wringing cannot stem its force. Despite the scars of war, Europe remains a great big museum for the world and America in particular, since we have so little of age. It is a treasure house of historical inspiration, a sculpture court of ornament and design, the source book of modern Western culture. It has done a great job of adapting itself to the twentieth century, making changes and modernizing where necessary.

The veal may not be quite as good in Italy as it once was; the saleslady in Paris may not say *"Oui, monsieur"* with the same charming lilt to her voice as formerly; the valet at Claridge's may not unpack the luggage as in yesteryear; but two things remain supreme and unchanged: the London cab and cabbie.

Habit de Sculpteur

Se vend à Paris Chez Chiquet   Rue St Jacque près les Mathurins   Avec Privil. du Roi

12

The Collector's Eye

Museums and stores have much in common: they both have the obligation to render a visual service to those who enter. The museum's function is to exhibit its collections in a manner to gratify and educate its visitors, and to provide opportunities for study and research to students and serious scholars with interests varying from aesthetics to techniques. The aim of stores is to satisfy the spoken and unspoken desires of the customers and to sell to them; to accomplish this objective, they, too, must display their assortments in a pleasant and attractive manner. In addition, stores have an educational role, for today's looker becomes tomorrow's buyer. Each has a lot to learn from the other.

Both institutions have understood the necessity to make their presentations easy to see and comprehend, so as to make visits exciting adventures. The similarities between the two go even further. Some of each are gargantuan in size, others are smaller and closer to the human scale. The very large museums, like the department store, have found it desirable to departmentalize their collections to avoid the hazards of overwhelming their patrons.

Whenever I travel, I prepare a list of the museums in the various cities I am going to visit and put them on my agenda. If there are any places on my itinerary that I have not been to previously, I'll go to the museums before I do anything else, for they provide a key to the understanding of the history and culture that nothing else does so well. In preparation for our foreign Fortnights, museums have been invaluable as sources of design and information. I've seen museums in most parts of the world, and some I've liked better than others. I am more than willing to share my opinions, on the condition that they must be regarded as opinions and possibly prejudices, and not as pronouncements.

In no way is this meant to be a compendium of the museums of the world, but rather some personal observations on those which have given me the greatest amount of pleasure and which I enjoy revisiting. The encyclopedic museums are wonderful and essential as storehouses of our artistic culture and history. In this category, I place such institutions as the Metropolitan Museum, the Louvre, the Hermitage, the British Museum, and the National Gallery in Washington, but I don't particularly enjoy them. I go to them to see specific exhibitions, but they tire me and I don't tarry long.

Of course, no art education is complete without a visit to the giant museums, but my preference is for some of the smaller, more intimate museums with specialized collections and a few of the very large ones that have unique examples or collections of particular artists. For instance, the Kunsthistorische in Vienna has a large share of all the Brueghels in the world, and if you want to know Brueghel, you must go there to see them. Since Spain was part of the Hapsburg Empire, an equally large number of Brueghels were sent to the members of the royal family residing in Spain, and are housed in the Prado. If you want to see all of these you must go to both places. The same holds true for paintings by Velázquez and Goya. When the former did court paintings or portraits of members of the royal family, he made them in duplicate, so that the family in Vienna could share the enjoyment with those who lived in Madrid. The collection of Goyas in the Prado is so comprehensive that it is impossible to appreciate the genius of that painter without visits to that museum, badly lighted as the pictures may be.

There are good small museums and poor ones, the point of difference being mainly in the quality and taste of their collections. A museum which acquires and accepts as gifts will possess more that's worth seeing than the museum which buys less discriminately. A top-quality painting by a lesser artist is a better buy than a poor painting by a great name, although very large museums may choose a secondary work to round out a definitive collection of a certain artist. It's particularly rewarding to see a museum where there is evidence of a selective eye, where a large number of the objects are of gem quality.

The Kimbell Museum in Fort Worth is the next to last museum designed by the late Louis Kahn, who created one of the most beautiful and nonoverpowering buildings in the art world. Aside from a few paintings owned by the late Kay Kimbell and his wife, the collection represents the selectivity of a single individual, the director, Richard Brown. The trustees of the foundation, none of whom had a strong art orientation, charged him with the responsibility of building the collection and backed him with one of the largest acquisition budgets in history. He had six years in which to do the task, from 1966 to 1972, a period, incidentally, when all art objects reached new price peaks as the result of inflation.

In the normal course of affairs it would take a museum thirty years to collect the art objects that Brown had to gather in a half dozen, and it is reasonable to believe that given the longer period, he would have improved his selections in many cases. The general overall quality is good though not brilliant, but I think it came off well—considering the impossibility of the challenge. The collection contains examples of nearly all eras of Western and Oriental art, from a Cycladic idol to a Matisse and from an Aztec sculpture to a Chinese handscroll of the Yüan Dynasty.

My ideal of a small museum is one with a fine collection that can be viewed in about an hour's time and with a pleasant eating facility, so that after a bit of refreshment, the galleries can be reviewed. The Kimbell is of that size, with an adequate restaurant area. The food, such as it is, leaves much to be desired for an institution of the stature of the Kimbell and the activity it generates. It would do well to emulate the food service of the nearby Dallas Museum of Art.

The Dallas Museum has made dramatic strides in the past

ten years, with a conscious effort by two successive directors to upgrade its collections. It has authoritative strength in African sculpture, pre-Columbian gold, textiles, and terra-cottas, and twentieth-century and contemporary American art. With the exception of a few good Impressionist paintings and a scattering of Classical and Oriental objects of quality, the museum has great areas of weakness in paintings and sculpture prior to the twentieth century. The important fact about the Dallas Museum is that it has a sense of direction and a long-range plan for accomplishment.

Of the medium-size museums I have visited, I like the Albright-Knox Art Gallery in Buffalo; the McNay in San Antonio; the Nelson in Kansas City; the Amon Carter Museum of Western Art in Fort Worth; the Worcester Art Museum; the Wadsworth Atheneum in Hartford; the Walker Art center and the Minneapolis Institute of Arts. With the exception of its collection of Impressionists, I find the Houston Museum of Fine Arts dull, the Virginia Museum in Richmond spotty, the High Museum in Atlanta, third-rate. Miami should have a great museum as a tourist attraction, if for no other reason; but it has only the Lowe Art Gallery at the University of Miami in Coral Gables which is nice but not strong.

The San Antonio Museum is housed in a wing of the nineteenth-century Lone Star Brewery. Its collection is modest, but the rehabilitation job by the Cambridge 7 was done with wit, imagination, and taste.

Personal collections of great collectors, preserved intact either in museums of their own or in separate rooms of the larger institutions, hold great fascination for me. I find it interesting to get an insight of the collecting proclivities of others, and to observe the changes in their taste and the scope of their interests. For those reasons, I find myself returning frequently to the Phillips and Dumbarton Oaks collections in Washington; the Arensberg and the Barnes in Philadelphia; the Gardner in Boston; the Lehman and the Frick in New York; and Winterthur in Wilmington. Although the Hirshhorn Gallery in Washington contains splendid examples of contemporary art, it suffers from a lack of careful editing, stemming from the desire of Mr. Hirshhorn to have everything, both the best and the unimportant. The circular building that houses the collection is no more successful than most other round buildings, but every architect seems impelled to do one at some point in his career, despite the predictability of failure. The Hirshhorn suffers from a lack of transition stages between the various sections of the collection; the flow is continuous, giving the weary visitor not a moment's respite before having to look at more art of another artist or period. The collection is more and more of the same, and the architecture merely adds to the confusion.

There are a number of specialized museums throughout the country which are delightful to visit because their exhibitions are small but expert, such as the Textile Museum and the Museum of African Art in Washington, Asia House, the Corning Museum of Glass, the Museum of the Southwest (Indian art of the Southwest) in Los Angeles, and the Museum of International Folk-Art in Santa Fe, recently enriched by the Alexander Girard Collection.

There are three large museums outside of the United States that have overcome the penalties of size by innovations of layout, making it easy for visitors to see and understand their collections. The Anthropological Museum in Mexico City rates at the top of the list for its architectural design, its organization and explanation of the exhibition material, and its display techniques. Chronological and geographical charts of the various cultures are most helpful in keeping unfamiliar names in proper sequence and location. In addition, on the second floor, displays of contemporary Mexican life are located immediately above the archaeological exhibitions, facilitating the correlation of the present with the past. The huge atrium, with its giant fountain, permits the visitor to step from a gallery into the fresh air, take a smoke, and rest the eyes before moving to the next salon. A reading knowledge of Spanish is helpful, for none of the descriptive material is translated into English.

Next in order, in my opinion, is the Israel Museum in Jerusalem, which shows everything from Biblical archaeology to contemporary art. The strength of the museum is its wonderful archaeological material of the Middle East, which has been supplemented now by the exchange of duplicates for archaeological objects of other countries. Following the contour of the hill on which it is located, the museum was built in a series of terraces at different levels with one complete wall of glass that provides a huge panoramic view of part of Jerusalem. There is a graciousness and a flow to this museum emanating from the architectural design. The introduction of such vast amounts of daylight and exterior scenery is a welcome and successful innovation to relieve traditional museum ennui.

The third large museum of distinction is the Dahlem of West Berlin. It, too, is a postwar building of contemporary design, but its most noteworthy features are the quality of its art works and its superb job of presentation. Among its prized possessions are its Rembrandts, located in a single room for easy viewing and comparison, and Vermeer's *Lady with a Pearl Necklace*. It has great Oceanic, African, pre-Columbian, Islamic, and Oriental collections, with large individual halls for each one. The works are dramatically lighted and displayed in a manner that would rival the best installations of a world fair exhibition. At the entrance to the pre-Columbian section, there is a glass case showing the stratification of the soil over a two-thousand-year period, embedded with small terra-cotta figures to indicate the different artifacts found at hundred-year intervals. This museum not only exhibits well but it understands how to teach well.

Europe is the home both of great museums and of extraordinary special exhibitions. These may be organized as a historical celebration or as a retrospective of a single artist or on a theme inspired by a culture, a nation, or an idea. In Paris, every year, there are four or five monumental shows at the Grand Palais or at l'Orangerie. In London and Zurich and in every major city of Europe, particularly in the spring and summer, there will be exhibitions of such nature. They are great attractions to lure the profitable tourist trade, so the governments finance them.

In addition to the big shows, there is so much art to see that it is nearly impossible to cover them all. In England, of the small to medium-size museums, I like the Tate in London, the Fitzwilliam at Cambridge, and the Ashmolean at Oxford. In Paris, there is the Rodin; the collection of Monet water-lily paintings, the Nymphéas, at l'Orangerie; the Impressionists at

Le Jeu de Paume; the Marmottan Museum with its Monet collection. In Rome, the Villa Giulia was among the first museums to exhibit antiquities in a modern setting by displaying its Etruscan bronzes and terra-cottas on contemporary lucite stands. In West Berlin, there is the Egyptian Museum that has the famous painted sculpture bust of Nefertiti, along with a small collection of the finest Egyptian material I have seen anywhere. Since I have a keen interest in primitive art, whenever I go to Zurich, I always go to the Rietberg Museum, which houses a discerningly selected collection of non-European art originally gathered by the connoisseur Baron E. von der Heydt. Since his gift of the collection to the city, it has been augmented by a number of contributions from other sources. This collection of about two thousand pieces is a splendid capsulization of the artistic expressions of the people outside of Europe over a period of five thousand years.

A week in Holland is very rewarding to those with an interest in art, for it is possible to cover the major and minor museums of almost the entire country in that time. It's immaterial whether you stay in Amsterdam, Rotterdam, or The Hague, for each of these cities is within one hour or less driving time from any of the others. Two days should be devoted to Amsterdam to see the Rijksmuseum, where Rembrandt's *Night Watch* hangs, along with the best examples of the Dutch masters of the seventeenth century; the adjacent Stedelijk Museum, with its fine collections of nineteenth- and twentieth-century art; and the new Van Gogh Museum, which has united under one roof the collections of that painter, previously divided between the Stedelijk and the Kröller-Müller museums. It has over four hundred van Gogh paintings and drawings.

On another day, on the way to The Hague, it is easy to drive via Haarlem to visit the Frans Hals Museum, which contains not only the paintings of Hals, a native of the city, but important works of the other great Dutch seventeenth-century artists. The Gemeentemuseum in The Hague has a modern collection with a large representation of the early works of Mondrian and other de Stijl artists. There is the Bredius Museum with a fine group of paintings and objets d'art amassed by Dr. Abraham Bredius, an illustrious Dutch art historian, who left his collection, along with his charming seventeenth-century house in which it is installed, to The Hague. Last and most important of all is the Mauritshuis, second only to the Rijksmuseum for its superb collection of Dutch and Flemish paintings, which include notable examples of Rembrandt, Vermeer, Steen, and Rubens. The building, a fine example of Dutch Renaissance architecture, was designed for Prince John Maurits, and after his death it was used as a royal guest house until 1921, when it became a museum. This has nothing to do with art or museums, but on the way back to Amsterdam, it is worth a half-hour stopover to see Madurodam, the world's tiniest village, encompassing a ten-acre plot on which everything from historic sites, homes, churches, railway systems, docks, and an airport have been reproduced on a scale of 1:25. What's more, everything works. Adults as well as children can enjoy it.

One of the most memorable experiences I have ever had was the sight from a plane window of the Holland tulip fields in full bloom. As the plane approached Schiphol, the national airport of Holland, it banked several times to give us a better view. The vista was a riot of color, which was like looking down on a giant Impressionist painting. But this sight and the tulip gardens of Keukenhof are thrills that come only in late April and in May when the tulips are at their peak, which makes a great bonus for the art traveler fortunate enough to be in Holland at that time.

The Kröller-Müller Museum near Otterlo in the Hoge Veluwe National Park was built just before World War II to hold a superb collection of paintings, drawings, and sculptures collected by Mrs. H. Kröller-Müller. It includes a very important section of the art of the late nineteenth and twentieth centuries. Until recently the largest group of van Gogh paintings in the world were shown there—some 270—but as mentioned, these have been transferred to the new Van Gogh Museum in Amsterdam. There is a delightful sculpture garden behind the museum with works of leading contemporary artists, including a white-plastic sculpture which floats in the pond on a tether, undulating with the breeze and movement of the water. It is called *The Swan*, by Marta Pan, a Hungarian now residing in Paris. A similar sculpture now floats in front of the new I. M. Pei–designed municipal center in Dallas.

Rotterdam was virtually wiped out by bombing and fires during the war, and, as a result, the city planners had the opportunity to design a completely new city on the site of the old one, and to provide green areas and open spaces which would have been impossible to accomplish under any other circumstances. Zadkine was commissioned to create a huge sculpture, *Memorial to a Destroyed City*, located at the center of the most heavily bombed section. The Boymans-van Beuningen Museum is rich in seventeenth-century Dutch and Flemish great names, but, in addition, has a fine collection of modern sculpture.

A traveler will have no difficulty in visiting these various cities and all the museums mentioned in one week and still have time left over to go to the cheese market, the flower auctions, the nearby islands, and even parts of eastern Holland.

When I drove from Holland to Brussels, I particularly wanted to see Middelheim, for I was intrigued with the idea of the "Open Air Museum for Sculpture," which is located in this suburb of Antwerp. Examples of all the great modern sculptors from Europe and America are to be found in this pleasing setting. It has, among others, a cast of the Henry Moore *King and Queen*. The other museum in Belgium that I could visit many times is the Tervuren, which specializes in the art of the Congo. Since Belgium, at one time, possessed a large part of the Congo, it was only natural that the region attracted national interest and that examples of its art would be brought back by settlers and expeditions. This museum renders a unique service to collectors which no other that I know about has ever attempted. If a buyer is interested in purchasing a piece of Congo sculpture from a local dealer, he can take it to the Tervuren and the museum will issue, for a nominal fee, a certificate either denouncing it as a fake or authenticating it as genuine with an opinion as to age and condition.

Four other museum experiences stand out in my memory. I have visited these institutions only once, but I should like to return for a second look. One is the famous Topkapi Palace Museum in Istanbul with its superlative collection of Islamic porcelains and artifacts from the Mogul empire. I recall it as having been breathtaking. The second museum is of quite a different sort, one that could be characterized as being undramatic but full of charm. That is the Louisiana at Humlebaek, outside of Copenhagen. It is devoted to twentieth-century Danish painting, sculpture, and crafts, supplemented with loan exhibitions from other countries. The collection is not great, for Denmark doesn't have that many great artists, but it is an honest effort to show the best the country produces artistically, and with pride and style. Its name puzzles most Americans, who find it difficult to establish a connection between it and the State of Louisiana. There is no connection; it was named by the nobleman who had built the original house on the site now occupied by the museum. He had married, successively, three wives, all named Louise. Hence the name Louisiana, which has stuck with the museum.

The third is the Amano Museum in Lima with the most perfectly selected collection of pre-Columbian textiles, terracottas, and gold I have ever seen. This is a private collection in a museum setting which is open to the public on certain days of the week, and it was assembled by a Japanese couple, Mr. and Mrs. Amano. The collection is not large, compared to others in Lima, but every piece is of the choicest quality, and is displayed with the precision and discipline characteristic of the Japanese. I suspect they must have three pieces in storage for every one shown. The textiles are exhibited on transparent plastic panels in a well-lighted vitrine, beneath which are metal tray drawers holding additional pieces of similar design motifs. Attendants in the room watch the interest of the visitors and as soon as they detect particular attention to a fabric on display, they come up and ask, "Would you like to see others of this type?" They then pull out the appropriate drawers to reveal dozens of fabrics of all the different Peruvian cultures. No museum with which I am familiar offers a similar voluntary service. If I were to name the one most perfect museum I have ever visited, it would have to be the gemlike Amano.

My son and daughter had stumbled on an ethnological

museum in the small town of Tenri, about a half-hour drive from Nara. They recommended it highly; so, on my first trip to Japan, I made it a point to go there. Imagine a town of about sixty thousand population with an ethnological museum larger than any in San Francisco, Los Angeles, Houston, Dallas, or St. Louis. It had Egyptian, Persian, Greek, Indian, African, pre-Columbian, American Indian, and Oriental collections in depth. It was like a miniature edition of the Museum of Natural History. But why in Tenri? The answer is simple. In 1838, Miki Nakayama founded the Tenri-kyō religion, which was accepted by the Japanese government as an independent sect in 1908. One of her descendants, the Reverend S. Nakayama, formed a permanent collection of ethnological objects, later adding archaeological articles, to help in the education of members of the church, their children, and presumably the missionaries. In time a museum was built to house the collection and to facilitate the study of foreign culture and customs, with the avowed purpose of bringing the world closer and to establish better understanding between nations and peoples.

From my many references to museums with ethnological and archaeological emphasis, it may seem easy to discern the fields of my particular interest. That is partially true, for though a part of my modest collecting activities has been in African and pre-Columbian objects, I am attracted to most areas of artistic creativity, with the exception of early religious painting, which leaves me cold. I can enjoy a single gallery of Adorations, Ascensions, and Madonnas in the Uffizi and one of icons in the Tretyakov in Moscow, but seven consecutive galleries of either are too much.

Frequently, I lecture on the subject of "The Care and Cultivation of Collectors"; and, without exception, the question is asked, "How do you start collecting?" My answer is very simple: first, you have to want to collect; second, you must learn some elemental facts about the field in which you want to collect; third, you must train your eye as rigorously as a coach trains a fighter; fourth, you must be able to enjoy the process. Some collect out of a sense of snobbery, to impress others. In all honesty, I think I was slightly motivated by snobbery when I first started collecting forty years ago. At that time, collecting in Dallas was a bit esoteric and I enjoyed being referred to as "that fellow who collects crazy masks from Africa," but soon that gave way to genuine pleasure as I studied and began to learn from books, museum exhibitions, and from the process of buying. The actual act of a purchase is a strong educational force; real experience begins when you have put your own money down to buy something. If you make a bad purchase, which happens to all collectors, you learn from that.

When a collector develops both knowledge and a sense of taste, he is said to have an "eye." Many times I have visited galleries for several days without seeing a thing with appeal, and it made me wonder if my taste had become so jaded that nothing looked good. About the time I began to despair, I would come across something that excited my eye, a work that said, "Buy me!" Then I knew my eye wasn't off. Some buy art as an investment and they may have done very well; I never have bought with that motive. I have acquired what I have liked within the limitations of my purse; if my purchases have increased in value, I don't like them a bit more.

My best advice to all beginners in the collecting field is the same I have given about buying jewels and furs: find a reputable dealer, tell him what you like and can afford to spend, and put yourself in his hands. He is not likely to let you down. As you progress in the accumulation of knowledge, you can then afford to be more venturesome and take a flier on your own judgment. The danger a young collector faces is the temptation to buy junk art, because it's pretty or familiar. Though it may be inexpensive, junk art is almost always genuine, and genuinely bad. As the collector becomes more experienced and affluent, he becomes attracted to more expensive art, and the more costly it is, the hazards are greater that it may be a fake. It doesn't pay to forge an inexpensive object, but the rewards for counterfeiting an expensive piece can be great. That is a cogent reason for doing business with an established dealer who guarantees the authenticity of anything he sells and can be easily located if you have to come back to him.

Quality in art depends on two factors: first, the skill of the craftsmanship, how well it is carved, painted, executed; second, the validity of the artist's idea and concept. Value is determined by these factors plus a number of others. Here are some of them. Value may be enhanced by the provenance of the work; if it came from a famous collection, it will cost more. Value may be affected by the fashion of the moment; if it is in the mainstream of the current movement, it will be worth more. Value may be artificially manipulated by the efforts of one or more dealers collusively holding the supply of works off the market to get higher prices, or "orderly marketing," as it is called in the trade. Value may be influenced by a major exhibition and by spontaneous or contrived publicity. None of these factors give any assurance that the values established will hold; only time has that answer. That's another reason to buy what you have learned to like.

Some final bits of advice. Don't try to buy directly from artists. If you do, you will undoubtedly make an emotional decision based on sympathy, personalities, or the inability to say "no." Meet the artist after your purchase if you must. Certain dealers, particularly those in antiquities, will give a discount if you buy a lot of three or more pieces. Don't be tempted; buy fewer, buy better. A true collector never worries about where a painting can be hung; he knows that if he really likes it, he'll find a place.

I've always had art objects in my office for two reasons. I like to be surrounded by beauty wherever I may be, even to the point of bringing two of my favorite paintings to the hospital when I went in for surgery, and I have tried to select works which demonstrated the ingenuity of artists in the use of new materials to solve creative problems, which I thought would be stimulating to buyers. Frequently, when I heard complaints about the staleness of the fashion markets and the lack of anything new and exciting, I would point to a collage made of thin leather, or a construction made from nylon thread in multicolors, or a design made from nailheads, to demonstrate the ingenuity of creative artists in solving problems much like their own.

My office visitors usually showed interest in the art, but I never gave much thought as to the influence it might have on them, until I read *On Women & Power*, by Jane Trahey, who wrote, "A lot of my hungers and desires to own good paintings, collect great books, travel like crazy, and do my own thing generated while sitting in Stanley's office working out the weekly advertising schedule." Perhaps it's rubbed off on many more who just haven't gotten around to writing a book yet.

My knowledge of art helped me a great deal in business. The training of my eye helped me to establish higher standards of beauty and quality in merchandise, store architecture, advertising, and display. I have used art for commercial success, and art, in turn, has enriched the quality of my life by constantly leading me to the best.

Habit de Vigneron.

A Paris, Chez N. de L'Armessin, Rüe St Jacques, a la Pome d'Or.   Avec Privil du Roy.

13

The Future for Fine Quality

An attempt to forecast the future for fine quality is as difficult as trying to predict what a twenty-five-year-old beauty will look like when she is sixty, but it's worth a try.

Obviously, human life on earth is going to be affected by the type of economic system prevailing, but, barring a proletarian dictatorship which reduces everything to a standard of uniformity for one and all, I find it difficult to conceive of a time when there won't be a premium for the best. As long as there are different sizes of oranges, there will be customers willing to pay more for the largest and juiciest. I find it equally difficult to imagine either the French or Italians living under an egalitarian society, whatever parties may be in power. Even in Russia, there is indication that those in top governmental positions get the preference for the best of what is available.

But the demand for the finest will still exist; the problem is going to be to find it. As James Laver wrote in *Taste in Fashion,* "It is useless for Puritans of every period to sigh for the simple, uncorrupted manners of their fathers. Every age has enjoyed what luxury it could, and the degree of its luxury has been, almost always, the measure of its civilization."

Of one thing I'm sure: when people have money, they upgrade their automobiles and clothing and indulge in whatever luxuries of life they can afford. I saw this happen in

The Future for Fine Quality

1939, when war preparations put thousands back to work after several years of unemployment. The women riveters wore overalls on the assembly line, but they came to Neiman-Marcus after work to buy something "nice" for their leisure hours.

I have watched men and women buy a wide variety of products for many years, and I have frequently heard them ask: "Is this the finest?" or, "Is this the best?" I've studied their motives for wanting the finest or the best, and I have found them varied. To some, it's a matter of prudence, for they have found the best may last longer; to others, it's a point of pride, of leadership, of self-distinction. Another group gets sensual and aesthetic satisfaction from the actual handling and ownership of the best. And, of course, there are those who are trying to "keep up with the Joneses" and buy the best because it's the snobbish thing to do.

The growth of $50,000-plus family incomes in the United States is dramatic evidence of a broadened distribution of wealth and enlarged disposable spending power. There is little reason to believe these motivations won't continue, and unless the tax system becomes completely confiscatory, there will be disposable income with which to buy the best products and services available, the choicest hotel accommodations, and seats on the fifty-yard line.

Snobbism is not one of the more attractive human characteristics, but it's a fact of life that can't be ignored. It exists at all levels of the social structure and is the subject of a witty, satirical book, *Snobissimo,* written by the French writer Pierre Daninos. He tells a story which must be the ultimate in snobbism:

It happened a few months ago to the most illustrious saddle-shop owner of our capital. I do mean the one whose name ennobles a plain duffel bag and who has in his store, especially in December, the greatest density of snobs per square feet—not only because it is gift-giving time but it is also the moment to buy the refill of the famous pocket calendar covered in Russian leather, which has become such a status symbol that it would not be appropriate to enter any appointment in any other calendar.

Our famous saddle maker had in his service, and for quite a

while, a butler who was offered by a neighbor (living on the avenue Foch and using his chef as intermediary) double the salary he was getting at avenue Bugeaud. This good "stealing" soul knew through his *"cordon bleu"* that the prestige of the avenue Foch address had always tempted our man since the beginning of his career. He was about to reach a new plateau of income with wages of a squadron leader, but he did not accept.

The most surprised of the three was not the one you might think—the one offering big money—but the saddle-shop owner who knew, still through the kitchen channels, how much gold was offered his pearl.

Our shop owner finally asked his butler how he could, despite his loyalty, turn down such an offer. The butler, after pointing out his attachment to Monsieur and his children, finally came up with the truth with the following remark, "And then after ten years at your service, could Monsieur see me working for people who are in plastic?" This proves that one can carry the nobility of leather in a butler's heart.

The newly rich "plastics" man of the avenue Foch has not yet recovered.

After that, can you say that money buys everything?

Certain articles of merchandise become snob or status symbols and develop an extraordinary volume of business because of superb quality, such as Hermès scarves, or because they were avant-garde at one point in time, such as Gucci loafers and Vuitton handbags, or because of a society-personality endorsement, as in the case of Halston. Once established as status symbols, the life of these objects is perpetuated by the snob appeal they carry to the rest of the public because "they" are wearing them. These articles, in turn, become favorite gifts, as a result of being "in" and having a recognizable monetary value. The snob wants to be sure that the recipient understands how much the gift cost. The life expectancy of status symbols is unpredictable, but those I have mentioned have been around from fifteen to twenty years.

Snobbism is the explanation of store and designer labels, automobile-hood emblems. Never has a customer asked Neiman-Marcus to remove its label from the lining of a coat, but many have been the requests for a new Neiman-Marcus label to replace one that has become frayed or soiled. I've known of black-market operations in Neiman-Marcus labels with prices as high as $10 for coat labels. Stores have failed to recognize the emotional value of their own label to their customers and have been fighting a losing battle with their manufacturers who have pre-empted the best label locations in garments for their own brand identifications. Individual store labeling is difficult in today's mass-manufacturing process, but the stores have been patsies by allowing their suppliers to get away with label murder.

The demand for fine merchandise, from automobiles to furs, is greater than ever before, bolstered in part by the purchasing force of the buyers of the OPEC nations. I know of one small jeweler in Paris who has produced over two thousand Mogul-styled, jeweled dagger handles at an average price of $15,000. Obviously, these went to the Mideastern markets and not to the U.S. Midwest. A famous Swiss watchmaker has been forced to triple the size of his jewel-setting shop to take care of the orders for diamond-faced men's wristwatches for one of the princes of Saudi Arabia, who sends them as tokens of appreciation for small favors.

Unfortunately, much of what purports to be fine is not fine at all; it is merely an expensive simulation of the fine. You see this in the travertine-lined lobbies of expensive new hotels, which have narrow vestibules, paper-thin walls, shallow closets, and hollow doors of the same standards found in a Bronx housing development. Cruises on refurbished, renamed vessels are advertised as the "ultimate in luxurious living at sea," and many of them turn out to be nightmarish experiences on poorly air-conditioned, badly staffed, maritime-code-violating, old ships. Advertising attains its sorriest hour of public irresponsibility by the garbage it manufactures to sell "luxury" package tours for its hungry travel-agent clients. The words "best" and "luxurious" become the magic shibboleths copywriters bestow on a host of dubious products and services which are faint facsimiles of the genuine.

The only things that best and bigness have in common is the initial letter *B*, but General Motors, it seems to me, is one of the few giants which has been able to retain its perspectives, to maintain the quality levels of its respective divisions, and overcome many of the problems of size. Management defines its objectives with clarity, it delegates full operating responsibility to the heads of its product lines, and establishes a continuity between its divisions through the General Motors Technical Center. Recognizing that Cadillac is and has been the status-symbol car of the United States for many years, I was interested in trying to find out why it occupied this position. The answer turned out to be the same as the one I got when I investigated the Hermès scarves. Cadillac caught the public imagination early in the game with its V-8 engine and its dedication to quality, and it never lost it because it never compromised its quality. Anyone who drove a Cadillac was regarded as "having made it," and the ownership of one became part of the American dream. For many years, its engineering was progressive and its designing, both interior and exterior, was superior, except for those horrible years of the tail fins.

With the demise of the Packard, it was only when Ford, after several abortive attempts, launched the Continental that Cadillac has faced serious domestic competition. Rolls-Royce, with its limited production of a superb car, has offered little challenge; but Mercedes-Benz has become a serious contender for a share of the luxury-car market. It's a different kind of car to drive than either the Cadillac or the Continental, but it has its share of enthusiastic proponents who prefer the "harder" steering wheel that gives the driver a greater sense of feeling complete road control than does the "softer" wheel of American automobiles.

There is no doubt in the mind of Cadillac's management that GM top brass wants Cadillac to be the finest car made in the United States, if not in the world. Their charge is clear, and their efforts are concentrated on the manufacture of a quality product that will ensure their leadership position. If this objective is not accomplished, it's likely to be the fault of the mass-production system rather than of the management. Although many of the innovations first introduced in the Cadillac are subsequently appropriated by other divisions of GM, Cadillac gets no subsidy for its creativity from the parent organization. Cadillac must finance its expansion from its own profits.

Quality guidelines in automobiles are much the same as

quality in other products, except for the great degree of complexity in the car industry. It has to start with the quality of people in charge, with their absolute dedication to an idea, and their willingness to do all the things necessary for attainment. As one of their senior executives has said, "You can't inject quality into a product; it has to be built in." Cadillac's greatest challenge will come from the movement toward smaller cars, for it will be increasingly difficult to achieve a real and visible differential with the constraints on size, and to maintain its mystique for taste as well as quality.

The differences between cars of closely related grades are not unlike those between similar bundles of mink or between diamonds of approximately the same weight and color. Once you pass a basic high standard, then the differences in each grade upward are small and subtle, for which the buyer pays an extra price. Frequently I've heard people say, "After you leave the Oldsmobile or Mercury price range, you're simply paying for trimmings and decoration on the more expensive cars, like Cadillacs and Continental Mark Vs." It's true that you pay more, but you also get more in the refinements of finish, the additions to comfort and convenience, and advanced engineering concepts. The transmission and the brakes may be the same, but the quality of labor that goes into upholstering the seats, into the extra coats of paint, into the additional soundproofing, makes the difference between better and best. The premium the buyer pays for a Cadillac or a Continental is comparable to that paid for the top bundle of sables or for the ten-carat diamond certified as D-Perfect.

Unlike apparel manufacturing and retailing, the capital costs in the motor-car business are so great that the small, new producer can't even get into the game, much less survive. GM and Ford dominate the industry, but are fiercely competitive, both with each other and within their own corporate structures. They occasionally suffer from myopia, as in their reluctance to foresee the inevitability of the smaller car and of pollution control, but these failures can give us the consolation that these giant companies are operated by human beings with all their fallibilities and not by computers. Even as they fight between themselves and with the foreign makers for the mass market, there is no indication that they are slackening in their efforts to get their share of the luxury market in competition with Mercedes-Benz and Rolls-Royce. A greater amount of hand labor goes into the making of the Rolls, which permits many of the refinements the others don't possess, but its price is two and a half to three times greater.

Most of the large fine-quality specialty stores are now owned by the large department-store chains. I. Magnin is a division of Federated Department Stores. Saks Fifth Avenue is owned by Brown and Williams, a subsidiary of British-American Tobacco, and Neiman-Marcus belongs to Carter Hawley Hale Stores. All three of these groups are embarked on expansion programs that eventually could double the number of their existing units. Thus it might appear that retailing is well aware of the demand for fine-quality merchandise and is expanding its capacity to serve it, but, unfortunately, at some point, size and quality become antagonistic and quality becomes the loser. It seems to me that the godfathers of the respective parent organizations are going to have to do some individual soul-searching and make their own determination as to whether they want to run the *finest* group of fashion specialty stores or the *largest*. It has become increasingly apparent to me that they cannot do both.

The success of the fine-quality specialty store was built on the foundation of superior selections, the ability to create certain merchandise specialties of the house, fashion leadership, personalized service to the customers by well-informed and trained salespeople, and an authoritative owner-customer relationship. As a business expands into multi-units in widely separated cities, all of these qualities become diluted to the point of ineffectiveness. Adam Gimbel was the first to multiply his specialty store, and I remember asking him how he was going to compensate for the impersonalization of his business. His reply was that with the huge volume he was going to generate, he could afford to pay the highest salaries in retailing to buy the best merchandising and buying talent. His idea worked for a while but, eventually, the sheer size of the operation created its own inertia.

Specialty-store retailers failed to develop sufficient numbers of adequately trained, specialty-store-oriented executives. As a result, they were forced to go to the department stores for manpower, and in most instances they achieved not relief but disaster. The average department-store recruit failed to grasp the significant differences in the two types of retailing. Most of them attempted to downgrade the specialty-store quality to that of the department store, not only in merchandise but in the character and nature of the typical specialty-store services. Department-store success is predicated on its ability to move huge amounts of merchandise with only a modicum of service; a specialty store is dedicated to selling its merchandise in lesser quantities with maximum attention to the subtleties of presentation and delivery. The department-store bull has wrecked many a specialty shop, in the proverbial manner.

Unless the big specialty-store operators find a better managerial solution and until they show a willingness to radically update their internal personnel-development programs, a large portion of the fine-quality business will be siphoned off by independent small to mid-size retailers who have a clearer understanding of what the big-spending customers want for their money. Most of them will be happy to work for a 6 percent pretax profit plus the many perks a small business affords. Action begets reaction, and the whole trend toward bigness and depersonalization of big business, particularly retailing, may very well be slowed down by a customer demand for smallness and personal attention. The quality of rudeness in all phases of commercial life, here and abroad, can be charged against managements that are too busy with expansion and refinancing to require politeness as a prime requisite for employment.

I don't think bigness is necessarily bad, but in the process of growing big, retailing has failed to solve all of its problems with equal success. Specialty stores, in particular, have three major challenges. The first is to completely reorganize their personnel departments, which are forced to spend a disproportionate amount of time on compliance with government employment regulations. These are important, but they should not be allowed to interfere with the creative aspects of personnel management. They need to mount an intensive effort toward the identification and location of talent and to maintain a constant "open-to-buy" for people of extraordinary ability. Then, they must develop new methods of training future leadership in the fundamentals of goods and customers as well as in the computer sciences.

I am unaware of any store, or any business school, for that matter, that conducts a course or a series of lectures on "The Care and Treatment of Customers." I am referring to "customers" and not "consumers," for never in my retail experience have I ever seen a "consumer" enter a store. I've seen lots of "customers," for that's what they call themselves. Thus, it might be worthwhile to give more than passing attention to the "anatomy of the customer" and to investigate those things customers like and those they don't. The development of the whole consumer movement came about as the result of the failure of retailers and manufacturers to give adequate attention to the physical and psychological needs of the customer.

They must find a way to teach the principles of quality in both operations and merchandise as well as the techniques of quality control. The study and analysis of the elements of quality in a dozen varied products, conducted by authorities in each of the manufacturing fields, could prepare a trainee with a knowledge of how to approach the merchandise problems of any department. A student should be shown the standards to expect in a dress at five different price ranges and the manufacturing cost differentials between these ranges. The same exercise should be repeated in shoes, lingerie, men's shirts, cosmetics, and furs. A retired production man could open the trainees' eyes to what the "take-out man" does to a product after it is sold and before the manufacturing process begins. Every experienced retailer knows many of these facts, but he is usually too busy to teach his training department, which doesn't have the slightest knowledge about manufacturing construction or manufacturers' markups or quality standards.

Management needs to encourage executive trainees to stay in their jobs long enough to learn enough to be authoritative and to help them in their career planning. Many young executives are leaving the larger stores to go into smaller businesses where they feel they have a better opportunity for self-expression. This is an indication to me that the stores are failing to understand what it takes to give full job satisfaction to all of its young executives.

The second challenge lies in the field of merchandise selection and presentation. At the present time, stores are running the risk of boring their customers to death by showing the same merchandise to be found in every neighborhood department store or shop. This has come about as the result of the multiplicity of branch stores which overlap each other in almost every market, by pressures of the Federal Trade Commission against confinement arrangements, and by the lack of generalship on the part of specialty-store managements to overcome these problems. The last condition stems from a managerial poverty that most specialty stores have brought on themselves. Specialty stores must get away from the "me too" scramble for designer names and develop a carefully edited merchandise point of view based on its own interpretation of fashion trends and the validity of its own label. They must bring showmanship back to the floor presentation of the merchandise and get away from the mass-racking of garments which Robert Hall introduced thirty years ago and which the department stores have been doing ever since, a method guaranteed to depreciate the visible value of the merchandise to any discriminating customer. A store can't expect to sell fine-quality merchandise in this type of environment.

Specialty stores must generate more excitement; they need to provide the thrill of the unexpected. Rod Steiger, in an interview with William Wolf in *Cue* magazine about W. C. Fields, made a comment about the late great actor which applies with equal appropriateness to specialty stores: "I really miss Fields," Steiger said reflectively. "I guess what I miss most is his audacity. That's a quality of which we don't have enough in our life today. There is too much timidity. We need more of the irreverence that Fields brought, entertaining us at the same time."

Spontaneity is a quality we admire in the theater and in life. We recognize the necessity for a script, but we admire a performer's ability to depart from it to respond to an unusual situation. Some of the greatest comedy lines in history have been born in such manner. Many of the greatest humorists on stage and television screen attempt to create the impression of spontaneity, even when their acts have been carefully plotted in advance. All business, and particularly retailing, needs to cultivate this ability of fast reaction, for no organization or individual is so omniscient as to be able to foretell all events six months hence with complete accuracy. I grant the necessity for careful advance planning, but we should not become so immobile in our devout worship of the process that business leaders become timid about departing from approved programs. Like Steiger's comment on Fields, I miss business audacity sired by the need for fast improvisations to meet new conditions.

Third, and finally, a specialty store must learn how to have special merchandise created for itself alone. This requires ingenuity and taste on the part of the buyers, full commitment by the management to back up its buyers with adequate money to cover the investments, and the development of training skills to get the enthusiastic sales cooperation from a far-flung sales staff. It is meaningless to have exclusive merchandise of poor design and quality, but there is no greater booster to sales morale than to have a dozen items of beauty, originality, and exclusivity.

I know this can be done, for I have done it. I used to encourage buyers to tell me about articles they thought could be sold which were not being made. Sometimes it involved a commitment for more expensive fabrics than our manufacturers were willing to buy, in which case we would make the purchase directly or advance the money to the maker to order for our exclusive use. In that way, we had huge stocks of vicuña coats when our competitors had none, or pure silks or fine gabardines during a period of market shortage. Naturally, there were risks, for we had to tie up capital to back up these programs; but a riskless business is a dull one for salespeople and customers alike.

Once, on a New York trip, I failed to bring a cummerbund to wear with my dinner jacket and I didn't discover this until I was dressing to go to a dinner party, too late to get a replacement. It occurred to me that others might suffer similar embarrassment, so I asked our clothing suppliers to make a tuxedo trouser with an attached cummerbund, making it impossible to leave it behind. This innovation made a big hit

The Future for Fine Quality

with the clothing salesmen, who had something new in the way of a tuxedo that they could show to every customer with the assurance that they would not get the answer "I already have one." We quadrupled our formal-wear sales that season.

On my first visit to the bazaars in Istanbul, I became fascinated by the amber mouthpieces used for smoking the hubble-bubbles, the water pipes. They were varied in color, some banded in gold or cloisonné, all shaped very much like the onion domes of the Byzantine cathedrals. I selected one hundred of them from the stalls specializing in used smoking equipment and, after going through the expected haggling, I bought them without having the slightest idea what I was going to do with them. Flying to Paris, it occurred to me that they would make handsome handles for umbrellas or canes.

The buyer liked the concept and suggested we take them to England to have them assembled. "Where are the finest umbrellas made?" I asked. "In France, of course, but they are so much more expensive," she replied. "Then, let's not try to save twenty dollars and sacrifice these beautiful antique mouthpieces. There will be one hundred customers who will be delighted to buy the finest umbrellas in the world. There's always a market for the best, if it is the 'best.' " The umbrellas were superbly made and we sold every one for Christmas gifts for some of the most discriminating women in the country. We delivered not only a fine luxury product but an interesting story at the same time. This encouraged the buyer, so that on subsequent trips she visited secondhand dealers and bought all sorts of interesting antique bits and pieces which she used for handles and bag ornaments. It took a little extra time and it required extra selling effort to get the story across to her salespeople in the branch stores. Whenever buyers complain about how hard it is to develop creative merchandise, I remind them that if it were easy, all their competitors would be doing it, too.

Inspired by the success Hermès was having with its scarf collection, in 1955 I suggested to our scarf buyer that we might try originating our own exclusive scarves, using the paintings of contemporary artists and the designs from old engravings. For some years, I had been gathering a collection of colored engravings of the various trades by a French artist named de L'Armessin, who in the seventeenth century was portraying the various tradesmen in a somewhat surrealistic style. We selected six subjects and had them printed on the same quality of fabric used by Hermès. To reproduce the colors exactly the printer had to use seventeen different screens. He offered to cut his price by 10 percent if we would let him eliminate three screens and slightly reduce the weight of the silk. We replied that we wanted no changes made and would pay him 10 percent more than his initial price quotation. We featured the scarf in our 1955 Christmas catalogue at the then-very-high price of $16.95 and had a complete sellout. This led to the establishment of the Neiman-Marcus Library of Fashion, and each year we presented two or three new designs, with continuing success. The saleswomen loved to show them to visiting businessmen, who were delighted to be able to find a lightweight gift to take home with the assurance that it was something not available anywhere else in the world, "not even at Marshall Field."

Before the war the Japanese shops in San Francisco used to sell Chinese bankers' coats in kimono silks in a wide variety of unusual patterns. When the shops reopened six years later, they specialized in inexpensive, tourist-quality merchandise. I made up my mind that on my first trip to the Orient I was going to find some of these robes for which I thought there was still a demand. I searched all over Tokyo without success, until one day I found the fabrics I was looking for in the kimono section of the Takashimaya department store, but then I couldn't locate a maker who was willing to take an order for a mere fifty robes. I bought the fabric, though, and lugged it with me to Hong Kong, where I found a small producer who was delighted to make fifty bankers' coats from my fabric. There was some cloth left, so I had it cut into men's kimonos. When they arrived in Dallas, I showed them very proudly to the buyers and the salespeople, but they weren't overly enthusiastic about them. I recognized that with their lukewarm reception the garments were not going to be shown with any understanding and that they wouldn't sell. I thought I knew of some customers who still remembered the prewar robes, but I found that most of the Orientalists had died off. I finally sold most of them, after buying six of the robes for my wife and two kimonos for myself. All of which goes to show that all creative efforts aren't hits, and that the boss can be, and often is, wrong.

The development of exclusive items will not be sufficient to make the difference. Quality specialty-store chains will be forced into setting up manufacturing units to supply themselves with merchandise that is theirs alone. This can be a costly operation, but it is the only way they are going to be able to get any degree of exclusivity and gain a competitive e!ge over the department stores and small shops which all offer the same merchandise. If they don't overcome the problems of standardization, then the only thing they have to offer their customers is more of the same.

For better or worse, bigness is here to stay, and I think it is too late for legislation to have much effect on growth, unless it is in the form of restrictions on enlargement by acquisitions. The increased size of populations has forced hospitals to become larger, factories to diversify geographically, retail stores to have more branches; and it is unlikely that these trends will disappear unless there are fundamental changes relative to how and where people live, which possibly could occur as the result of the energy crisis. But even if that should happen, the world is still faced with more and more people and the necessity to deal efficiently with the problems they cause.

Gone are the days when there were many family doctors who would make house calls in any urban community. Such personal attention is a luxury no longer affordable or practical in today's medical world in which modern technological advances require the treatment of the patient at a facility that possesses electronic testing and monitoring devices too costly and large to be portable. From the standpoint of efficiency, a doctor can check daily on a dozen patients in a single hospital in a fraction of the time it would take to make house calls. One of the less fortunate results of this dramatic change in medical treatment is that many doctors are diagnosing tests and computer printouts rather than their human patients, many of whom miss the more personalized human relationships of the past. In this new era, doctors rigorously observe their midweek days off and hospitals do only emergency work over the weekends, but there is no evidence that any increase in the mortality rate has occurred as a result.

This dissertation on medical practices was made to give emphasis to the fact that many things in life are changing as the result of the size of the population and the consequent development of the computer to deal with these problems. This leads to a whimsical speculation: "What if the Lord had created IBM on the eighth day?" Man has great resistance to immediate change which is superseded only by his resistance to change from the previous change.

That's what is going on in retailing now. Conditions which made it possible to run personalized, high-service stores in the past are no longer prevalent, and never will be again. This calls for a new scenario, in which stores must find fresh solutions to satisfying their customers; stores must recognize that profits can be permanent only if satisfaction is rendered, and must be aware that the demand for quality is not only still alive but growing. Customers, in turn, should not be bashful in their insistence on the best, for, as Somerset Maugham wrote in *The Mixture as Before:* "It is a funny thing about life, if you refuse to accept anything but the best you very often get it."

Habit de Tourneur.

A Paris, Chez N. de Larmessin, Rue St Jacques, à la Pome d'Or.　　　Avec Privil. du Roy.

Epilogue

Since Wallechinsky and the Wallaces have done so much to popularize lists in *The Book of Lists,* and have given assurance that "everyone makes lists," I have decided to add my own.

The BEST THINGS List

Linen bed sheets at Claridge's
Oxxford suits
Texas pink grapefruit
Château Petrus '53
Kobe beef
Sydney oysters
Levi's
Crane's stationery
Galanos dresses
Self-starters in cars
Peter's mineral-handled forks and knives
Tarte Tatin at Maxim's, Paris
Valextra leather goods
Automatic watches (not digitals)
Häagen-Dazs coffee ice cream
Oranges Orientales at Le Grand Vefour, Paris
Espresso at Caffè Greco on the Via Condotti, Rome
Montecristo cigars
The New Yorker magazine
The Mexican food at the Shed in Sante Fe, New Mexico
Bic lighters
Flare pens
Teuscher's Chocolate Truffles
Carrées Chocolate by Sprüngli of Zurich
London cabs and cabbies
Old Madeira
Saul Steinberg
Bang and Olufsen hi-fi equipment
Joe Baum, Restaurateur
Sony
Sara Lee pound cake
Sacher torte
Mangoes
Walla-Walla Sweets (onions)

Wild Pecan Rice
The Water Pik
The Concorde
Kaiserschmarrn
Demels' in Vienna
Evian water
Holland tulip fields
New England fall foliage
MacNeil/Lehrer Report
The Art Institute of
    Chicago
Honda cars

Peugot peppermills
Chaco Canyon
Canyon de Chelly
Twelfth-Century Peruvian
    textiles
Mimbres Pottery
2nd Phase Navajo Blankets
Hermès neckties
Hermès printed scarves
The New York Times
Cellular mobile phone service
Vivoli ice cream in Florence

Less than the Best List

Hotel art boutiques
Fish and chips
Bourbon whiskey
Las Vegas
Imitation furs
Three-inch clogs
Instant coffee
Nylon-bristle toothbrushes
Dictating equipment
Retail advertising
Plastic toys
Seven-day "luxury" cruises
Home cooking
Single-width shoes
Unpinked dress seams
Women's slacks with
    smiling crotches

Teased hair
Frilled tuxedo shirts
Campaign promises
Pin-lever watches
The U.S. telephone systems
TV dinners
New York City taxi service
Street food vendors
Hotel room illumination
Auto-repair service
Household-appliance repair
    services
Nonvine-ripened tomatoes
Stock options
Heat-sealed "Easy-open"
    polyethylene cracker packets
Political campaigns

"I did it! I did it! I found a substitute for quality!"

MARCUS'S LAWS
or
Principles Not Taught in the Business Schools

1. When business is good, no employee is actually as good as he thinks he is; when business is bad, no employee is as bad as management thinks he is.*
2. Never underestimate the value of luck, but remember that *luck* comes to those searching for something.
3. Taste and quality can be self-taught.
4. The competitive system is the only one that assures the attainment of the best.
5. Customers are people; consumers are statistics.
6. The only proof of a successful meal or food product is the request for seconds.
7. The only thing that can be discovered about a new employee in the first six months is whether he is a fool or a knave.
8. Public service is the rental price you pay for your space on earth.
9. To achieve success, it is first necessary to get along with your boss.
10. Never divorce the boss's daughter (or son).

* First enunciated in *Minding the Store,* 1974.

Index